IT'S A GOD THING!

INSPIRING STORIES OF LIFE-CHANGING FRIENDSHIPS

LARRY BAKER WITH BECKY LYLES

WINEPRESS WP PUBLISHING

Photographs courtesy of Dove Studios, Cheyenne, Wyoming

Printed in the United States of America.

Packaged by WinePress Publishing, PO Box 428, Enumclaw, WA 98022. The views expressed or implied in this work do not necessarily reflect those of WinePress Publishing. Ultimate design, content and editorial accuracy of this work are the responsibilities of the authors.

Unless otherwise noted, all scriptures are taken from the Holy Bible, New International Version, Copyright © 1973, 1978, 1984 by the International Bible Society. Used by permission of Zondervan Publishing House. The "NIV" and "New International Version" trademarks are registered in the United States Patent and Trademark Office by International Bible Society.

ISBN 1-57921-283-2
Library of Congress Catalog Card Number: 00-100104

"Go to the street corners and invite to the banquet anyone you find." (Matthew 22:9)

DEDICATION

This book is dedicated, with great appreciation and gratitude, to our families who believed in us and our story, plus did more than their share of proofreading. Larry's children—Todd, Stephanie and Kimberly—were supportive from afar (Ohio and Japan) and Becky's children—Alissa, Toby and Brady—from nearby Wyoming.

A special thanks goes to Kimberly, who was a great help to her dad during rough times, and to Steve, Becky's husband of 26 years and our most enthusiastic, indefatigable supporter. Steve deserves extra kudos for all the dishes and laundry he's moved through the household machines during the creative process.

We writers have basked and blossomed in the warmth and blessing of our families' constant love and encouragement.

ACKNOWLEDGMENTS

Without the individual stories of each person in this book, there would be no book. Many, many thanks go out to those of you who allowed us to share your intriguing tales with the rest of the world. We appreciate your generosity and your honesty!

We also thank our friends who volunteered their proofreading and editorial skills for our project: David Balsinger, Lanny Carey, LaJeanne Gilmer, Joyce Havel, Barbara LaBarbara, Letha and Dan Nusz, Nancy Reinhardt, Bob Thompson, Pat Watkins and Cindy Weibel. Your input was an incalculable contribution to the final product and your kindness will not be forgotten.

The women in Becky's Bible study group, all contemporary Proverbs 31 ladies, prayed this book into existence. Professional photography was graciously provided by Becky and Roger Carey, owners of Dove Studios in Cheyenne, Wyoming. Tom Byington, president of First State Bank in Fort Collins, Colorado, offered publication and marketing advice. The owners of Cornerstone Christian Supply in Cheyenne, Denise and Mark Notz, contributed research expertise. And, much time and many talents were generously donated by the entire Ralph Watkins family of Fort Collins.

Other friends and family members, too numerous to mention, gave encouragement and guidance along the way. We are grateful to all of you and to God for your gifts of time, energy, and friendship. "Every good and perfect gift is from above . . ." (James 1:17*a*).

CONTENTS

FOREWORD

If I were to describe *It's a God Thing!* in one word, it would be *Wow!*

I know many of the people in this book and am thrilled by their stories. Through them, and the exciting changes which happened in their lives, you and I are encouraged to believe that change can happen in our lives, too.

I have also had the privilege of knowing Larry Baker for many years and have watched him live out his life with passion and integrity. He is not without fault, but has found a way to turn sorrow, rejection and pain into an attitude which produces energy in his life rather than depletion. He has remained positive and optimistic amidst some of the greatest challenges a person can experience.

We live in a demanding culture. Life pulls and tugs at us and sometimes even traps us. This book will inspire you to a new level of hope. You will laugh. You may cry. You will be touched by the truths found in these pages. And, you will be encouraged to hang in there one more day.

You will also learn what it means to be a friend . . . a true friend. Not just a voice in someone's life telling them what to do or how they should live. But, rather, a friend who accepts people the way they are and gently helps them reach their potential in life.

The individuals in this book were fortunate to have Larry become their friend. His friendship changed them forever. I am honored to be able to say Larry is also my friend. He has inspired me to be a true friend to others.

Dary Northrop, Pastor
Timberline Church
Fort Collins, Colorado

INTRODUCTION

Y ou gonna take a hit with us, Lar?" Nikki snickers
and glances at the young woman sitting next to her in
the front seat, then at me in the back seat. Knowing I won't
join them, the woman giggles as Nikki passes her the pipe.

But I'm not laughing. I feel trapped. I can't breathe. My
head is throbbing. My heart is pounding. And my mind is
whirling. *How in the world did I end up in the back of a car
watching strippers smoke dope?* I remember Nikki inviting
me to a party but can't recall her saying snowcaps would
kick off the evening's activities. *Get me out of here, God,* I
pray, *before the cops come!*

I lean forward. "Hey, Nikki, don't you think this is
kinda dangerous doin' drugs right here on the street?" She
responds with a string of profanity and reaches through
her open window to knock out the used drugs. Then she
begins to refill the pipe, starting with marijuana on the
bottom. Just as she's about to top it off with cocaine, she
cries, "Where's the ———— pipe screen?"

Despite the fact that it's 10:00 P.M. and despite her mini-
skirt, Nikki jumps out of the car and drops to her hands
and knees on the pavement. Still screaming obscenities, she

crawls back and forth beside the car, furiously scouring the asphalt with her long, enameled fingernails.

When she can't find the screen, she hops in the car and backs into the road, the tortured tires of her little blue Geo squealing in objection. Nikki flicks on the headlights, then crouches in the street again, this time illuminated by the car's lights. Now I'm really beginning to panic, though the other passenger is laughing hysterically.

I hang out the window and holler, "Nikki, what if the police come?" Her head snaps up. "——— the police!" she yells, glaring into the headlights. "I'm gonna find the ——— screen and I'm gonna party tonight!"

Chapter 1

MIRACLE MAN

Partying with exotic dancers was a new experience for me in 1993, a result of a unique friendship with a young college student named Nikki. Three dramatic events in my life had led to that friendship and would ultimately lead to many other remarkable relationships. The first incident occurred in the spring of 1989 in Fort Collins, Colorado when I was 43 years old.

I had risen early on a beautiful May morning and hurried to a nearby golf course to play a round before work. The sky was clear and bright, birds were singing, and the foliage sparkled from a pre-dawn rain. I reveled in the fresh air, sunshine and solitude, thanking God for such a magnificent Rocky Mountain daybreak. Then I reached the third hole.

As I swung my driver, I lost my footing on the wet grass and hit the ground hard. When I regained consciousness, I was instantly aware of severe back pain. Moments later, I realized I could not stand upright. I also realized I was alone on the course. Knowing it could be hours before anyone found me, I crawled the 400 long yards to my car, dragging my clubs behind me. Somehow, I managed to climb behind the wheel and drive home.

After I hauled myself into the house, I called Tari, my hazel-eyed bride of four months, at the beauty salon we co-owned. "I think I ripped some muscles in my back," I told her. "Could you cancel my hair appointments for a couple of days?"

"Do you want me to come home, Sweetheart?" she asked. I could hear concern in her voice.

"No, I'll be fine." The pain was intense but I was an ex-Marine and too tough for my own good. Plus, I didn't realize the extent of my injury.

Tari came home over her lunch break anyway. I was lying on the couch, chock-full of aspirin. Not wanting her to know how much pain I was in, I said, "You go on back to work, Honey. I'll be OK." However, when she returned at 5:30 that evening, I was on the floor, screaming in agony. Tari called an ambulance.

That was the beginning of a 26-day hospital ordeal. At first, the doctors couldn't find anything wrong and tried to send me home. But I refused to leave. The pain was still so excruciating I couldn't get out of bed. Plus, I'd black out just attempting to turn over.

Finally, after more extensive testing, my doctor came in, his brow furrowed. "You've ruptured a disk and it's pushing into your spinal cord," he explained. "We have to get it out right away."

They wheeled me in for emergency surgery immediately, saying, "You'll be fine, Mr. Baker. It'll take some rehab afterwards, but you'll be OK."

Several hours later, however, I awoke to bright lights blaring above masked strangers hovering over me and peering into my face like in a bad sci-fi flick. Yet, I could tell I was still in the operating room.

"Mr. Baker, move your legs!" muffled voices demanded. I tried. "Move your right toe, move your left foot!" I couldn't move anything. Then I heard someone say, "I don't know what went wrong but we have to operate again."

So they put me back under anesthesia and hollowed out a couple vertebrae to give my swollen spinal cord more space. When I awakened the next time, I was in a private room. Tari was beside my bed, her face white with worry.

It wasn't long before one of the neurosurgeons marched in. "Mr. and Mrs. Baker," he announced, "I realize you've only been married a short time, but you need to know Larry may be a paraplegic the rest of his life. He might never walk again."

With that, the doctor pivoted and strode out of the room. Shocked, Tari and I just stared at each other. We hadn't had a clue I could leave the operating room paralyzed.

Our lives were changed in an instant. Besides dealing with the trauma of a severely injured husband, Tari found herself running a large salon without her business partner. One night when she came into my hospital room I could see she was worn out.

I took her hand. "Honey, you're exhausted," I said. "I love it that you're here but I love you and I want you to go home and get some rest."

"Are you sure?" Tari asked.

I replied. "I love you and I think that's what you should do." So she kissed me, then left.

I will never forget that evening in the hospital. It was 8:30 or 9:00. I could hear televisions and muffled voices in the distance, people shuffling up and down the hallway; but my room was silent. I felt isolated and confined, trapped in a living nightmare. I was a lonely prisoner of my own body.

When I first became paralyzed, I was told that if I could move my toes or feet within 10 days, I might have a chance to recover the use of my limbs again. Well, 10 days had come and gone without one lower muscle moving. It was disheartening to know I no longer had control over my body or my life.

On top of that, earlier in the day a doctor had come in and said, "I'm sorry, Mr. Baker, but I have to take out your catheter. We've got to run some tests on your bladder." He knew the pain nerves still functioned, which made the process more than uncomfortable. After he removed the tube, with an apologetic shrug the doctor added, "We'll put this back in around 9:30 or 10:00 tonight."

I didn't want to go through that torture again, so after the doctor left I did pull-up after pull-up on the bar over my bed, hoping to stimulate urination before he returned. Groaning and sweating, I worked my upper muscles over and over and over, but to no avail. The urine cup on the bed stand still sat empty.

That night, as I lay staring at the ceiling, feeling discouraged and depressed, out of the stillness a quiet voice inside my head and my heart said, "OK, tough guy, what are you going to do now? You've called yourself a Christian for years but you've never put me first. You've always worked out your problems your way, handled life on your own. Yet, if this hospital burned down right now, you couldn't even get out of that bed. Who are you going to turn to now?"

At that moment, I realized I had always depended on myself. Although I'd become a believer while still a teenager, I'd never let God be Lord of my life. "God, I am so sorry," I said. "Will you forgive me? I promise I'll depend on you from now on." As I felt His compassion and His forgiveness flow over me, I pleaded, "I feel so helpless and alone right now. Will you please give me a sign you're with me, that you care about me and love me?"

Instantly, I felt an urge to urinate, which was an incredible miracle and display of God's love for me. I reached for the cup beside my bed, tears running down my face. Later, my neurosurgeon told me, "In all of your amazing progress, the biggest surprise was when your bladder began functioning again."

Rehabilitation therapy in the hospital was a daily ordeal. At every session, the therapists would say, "Move your left foot, move your right foot. Wiggle your left toes, wiggle your right toes." It became routine and rhetorical. Nothing ever happened.

One day, shortly after my bladder miracle, we were going through the usual regimen when the therapist suddenly said, "Mr. Baker, I think I saw your toe twitch!" At that moment, I knew I would walk again.

When I left the hospital 14 days later, however, I was still considered a paraplegic though I had slight movement in one foot and two toes. I had a long way to go and no one could or would predict the outcome.

Tari was a tremendous encouragement to me during the paralysis. One night she said, "Hey, Hon, we're going out to dinner." She bathed me, blow-dried my hair, put my best suit on me, and got all dressed up herself.

Then she helped me into the car and drove me to one of the nicest restaurants in town. As we pulled up, she joked, "We get to use a handicapped parking spot! I've always wondered what this feels like."

Not knowing how people would react, we rolled in with our heads high and had a wonderful, intimate evening together. We held hands, me in my wheelchair on one side of the table and Tari in her seat on the other. She looked me in the eyes and said, "You're the best looking guy in a wheelchair I've ever seen, Larry. I love you. This will not destroy us. It's just going to make us stronger. We'll make it through, no matter what."

I was convinced I would walk again but the medical professionals weren't as optimistic. "If it happens," they said, "it'll take at least six months." However, I was determined to speed up the process. After my second physical therapy session at home, the therapist said, "You're way ahead of schedule. Since you're obviously motivated and working really hard, I trust you to continue exercising on your own. Just call if you have questions."

Thanks to the healing power of God and hard work, I went from a wheelchair to a walker, to crutches, then a cane, and finally to walking on my own within seven weeks. Hospital staff members still call me *The Miracle Man*.

CHAPTER 2

LITTLE TOUGH GUY

My best friend was the source and the center of the next unsettling episode in my life. Jack cut hair at the station next to me and was married to my sister Julia. He was stocky, five foot, four inches tall and the typical little tough guy. A very likable person, Jack had lots of friends as well as a large clientele. He was always ready with a good joke because he liked to make people laugh.

People often commented that we thought alike and we talked alike. We were closer than brothers. Jack loved the Lord like I did and we regularly told each other, "I love you," something a lot of guys aren't able to do.

Every chance we got, Jack and I went fishing together. When I was in the hospital, he said, "Larry, we'll still do fun things. If I have to carry you from the car to the canoe, we're floating the North Platte this year." And he meant it. Jack epitomized the meaning of the word *friend*.

After he and Julia divorced, Jack walked away from God. He took the path a lot of divorced people do, looking for a quick fix via a convenient relationship which resulted in another marriage right away, a marriage that was a disaster from the very beginning. That miserable situation just increased his pain rather than relieving it and ended in another divorce.

Jack's messed-up life didn't make me love him any less. I was, of course, concerned about him as I watched him party and go through relationship after relationship which only added to his already bulging emotional baggage. I could tell he had a lot of repressed anger and was becoming depressed, although he didn't realize it.

At lunch one day I said, "Jack, Man, you've been the best friend I've ever had and I'm very concerned for you. In the last few months I have seen you madder than I've ever seen you before. When we're out driving around, you get extremely angry at other drivers for just cutting in front of us. I'm worried that if you keep pushing your pain down inside and don't deal with it, it'll come back to hurt you and those around you."

Jack looked away, then turned to stare me directly in the eye. "Larry," he said, "you're my best friend but I don't want to talk to you or anybody else about this. It's something I have to work out on my own. I'll do it my way and we'll never talk about it again! OK?"

"OK," I responded.

A couple years later, however, I noticed he was displaying suicidal tendencies and tried to talk to him about it but, again, he didn't want to talk. Then, early one morning shortly after that conversation, my best friend put a shotgun to his heart and pulled the trigger.

Although I had seen it coming, I couldn't believe Jack had killed himself. I screamed and cried that night like I hadn't since I was a baby. That was in the spring of 1990, about a year after my accident. It took me a long, long time to get over Jack's death and I was thankful I had learned to depend on my loving, caring God for comfort.

CHAPTER 3

STANDING IN THE GAP

Tari was a great joy and solace in my life, not only through the paralysis but as I grieved following Jack's death. She was also a wonderful companion, especially after my three children moved to Ohio with their mother, my first wife. I dearly loved Todd, Stephanie and Kimberly and missed spending time with them. Tari helped ease the pain of separation from my kids.

She and I had almost everything in common, were together constantly and had as much fun with each other as two people can have. One of Tari's funniest traits is that she combines or confuses clichés. I call them Tari-isms.

For instance, one time when we were attempting to pull out into a busy intersection, she said, "It's like the Kentucky Derby!" (instead of the Indianapolis 500). Another time, she said, "It's just not my bag of tea!" Sometimes she would say, "I'm just talking out loud." Tari kept me laughing and I adored her and her unique sense of humor.

Although we thoroughly enjoyed each other, in the spring of 1992—two years after Jack took his life—Tari shocked me by telling me she was leaving our marriage. She said she was in a bad place spiritually and emotionally due to painful issues from childhood and had gotten into some destructive habits. So she was moving to Arizona to make a new start. Her last words before she drove away were, "Larry, I love you but I don't love myself anymore. That's why I'm leaving."

Surviving a previous, unwanted divorce, enduring the paralysis and losing my best friend and my family did not prepare me for Tari's leaving. It was the most devastating thing I ever experienced. We were two peas in a pod. Everybody loved us as a couple. Even my children had said, "Dad and Tari will be together forever."

I had sensed Tari was struggling with personal issues for at least a year before she left. In fact, I'd asked her several times, "Honey, is something wrong?" She had always answered, "No, I'm just going through some stuff right now." So I knew there were problems but had no idea she was considering leaving our marriage and Fort Collins.

I'll always remember the night Tari drove out of town. I wandered back into our beautiful but empty house in a daze. Her smells and her touches were there, even her clothes and her cats, but not Tari. I paced the floor, tried to watch television, then finally trudged up the stairs to our empty bedroom and attempted sleep.

All night long I tossed and turned. When I'd finally fall into a fitful slumber, I'd reach over to the other side of the bed, then wake up realizing Tari wasn't there. I can't begin to express the pain I felt. My life seemed even more hopeless than when I was paralyzed.

Each time I awoke, I climbed out of the bed, got down on my knees and begged for God's help. And, in the midst of that dark night, I heard the voice of the One who had been so faithful to me. "Son," He said, "this is going to be tougher than the paralysis, tougher even than Jack's death.

If you're going to get through this, you'll have to stay closer to me than you ever have before."

I must have crawled out of bed a half-dozen times that night. "I can't bear this pain!" I would cry. And the Lord would reply, "With me, you can."

During the difficult months that followed, God gave me the strength to go to work every day and the fortitude to face Tari's and my co-workers, clients and friends. He helped me be a peacemaker with Tari's family and with mine. I spent a tremendous amount of time in prayer seeking God's will for all concerned, especially during early morning walks.

The Lord let me know I was not to follow the pattern so many people do after divorce. I was not to go out looking for temporary fixes through drugs or alcohol or cheap relationships. I wasn't supposed to hook up with another woman right away. He had a much better plan for my future.

His Spirit seemed to urge me to get into shape spiritually, emotionally and physically. So that's what I did. I spent hours reading my Bible. I wrote letters to Tari's parents, my mom, my children and others explaining that it wasn't a bitter divorce; it wasn't about people not loving each other. It was about unresolved emotional issues which had to be worked out. For physical fitness, in addition to the morning prayer walks, I lifted weights every day. I wanted to become a healthy, whole person again.

Some of my friends said to me, "Tari caused you a lot of pain. Just write her off and move on with your life." But God prompted me to do something they didn't understand. He asked me to not only forgive Tari but to be her best friend. She'd left her husband and all her friends behind. Her own family had difficulty understanding her actions. She needed someone to care—and that someone was me.

My hurt, my loss and my own needs were immense. Still, God said, *"Show Tari she is a great person who has some serious problems. Show her my unconditional love. Pray for her every day."* I knew I was supposed to "stand in the gap," as the Bible says, for Tari.

The Lord also told me, *"Don't selfishly pray for your own needs. Don't ever pray for her to come back. Pray for her healing and for my will in both of your lives. That's true love and that's what she needs to see. If you will put me first, if you will pray for her and not for your own desires, I will bless you in ways you never dreamed."*

CHAPTER 4

SPITFIRE

After the divorce and the liquidation of our marriage assets, I was 47 years old and felt like my best years were behind me. I'd had everything a man could want in life—a great family, good friends, successful businesses, beautiful homes and nice cars. And I'd lost it all. Twice! It seemed like my life was at a useless standstill.

But God hadn't forgotten His promise to bless me. Eventually, with a miraculous provision of funds, I was able to open a brand new salon in downtown Fort Collins. It didn't take long to fill the shop with youthful, energetic, talented stylists.

Fort Collins is a lively, upbeat, college town with lots happening, especially for the singles crowd. Much of that activity is centered in the historic downtown area, also known as *Old Town*.

The turn-of-the-century buildings in Old Town—now restored and converted into brick and brass microbreweries, choice restaurants, and novelty shops—are a combination of old world charm and contemporary chic. Red brick walkways rambling between the time-honored structures are topped with shade trees and flowers, ornate lampposts, metal benches and sunny, outdoor cafes.

From early morning into the late evening, Old Town hums with shoppers, power walkers, bikers, rollerbladers, young couples pushing baby strollers, professionals conducting business, and folks just strolling with their dogs or visiting over lunch on a restaurant patio.

My entrance into the Old Town singles society in 1993 was engineered by my stripper friend Nikki, a four-foot, 11-inch, 99-pound, 21-year-old. Nikki was a little thing but she was a dynamo who liked to make a big statement, which was especially obvious in her appearance.

She sported elaborate hairdos and lavish amounts of makeup and jewelry; her clothing was unique, exotic, and often short or tight or both. Plus, she was loud. Nikki cussed more than the proverbial sailor and truck driver combined. She demanded attention; Nikki liked things to go her way.

She was also a full-time pre-law student at Colorado State University. To finance her education, she drove 50 miles to Denver three nights a week to dance at the most famous strip joint in the region. Nikki didn't see anything wrong with taking her clothes off for a living.

After all, she was talented and attractive, with a petite figure, big brown eyes and long, honey-blonde hair. To her, strip dancing was a means to not only pay for her education but to live comfortably. She had a new car, new clothes, a new apartment full of nice furniture, and she lived a high-flying lifestyle.

One evening several months after Tari left, Nikki came in for a haircut. Her skimpy top revealed a bare midriff, her floral-print stretch tights fit like they were painted on, and she was as vocal as ever. Yet, like always, I enjoyed visiting with Nikki as I worked.

When I finished with the cut, she stepped out of the chair, put her hand on her flower-covered hip and demanded, "Is

Tari coming back home?" Nikki was not one to beat around the bush. She just wanted to know.

"No, Nikki," I answered, "it doesn't look like she is."

She gazed at me with a puzzled expression, then cocked her head and asked, "Hey, you want to go out with me some time?"

I was so astonished, all I could do was stare back at her with my jaw hanging open. I was old enough to be her father; I was a family man, a church-going man, a business-man of many years. And here was this gorgeous little stripper asking, "Do you want to go out with me?"

Finally I blurted, "Sure, why not. Who wouldn't want to go out with you?"

Nikki grinned. "Let's go to dinner tomorrow night," she said. "I'll meet you over here about seven and we'll get some seafood."

So the next evening we went to dinner together. As we sat in the restaurant, eating and visiting, something happened to me. Suddenly I saw that sassy little spitfire through the eyes of Jesus. I no longer saw her as an exotic dancer who cussed too much; instead, I saw her as a tremendous person and as someone God loved.

We had a three-hour dinner and talked about everything. At the end of the evening I realized the attraction we had for each other had nothing to do with the physical, only the spiritual. I reached across the table, put my hand on top of Nikki's and said, "You know, Nikki, I think we're going to be really good friends."

Her expression turned serious as she pulled her hand away. "Don't count on it, Larry. I don't make friends easily. I've been disappointed by a lot of people in my life and I don't usually keep friends. But," she added with a smile, "we'll hang out some more."

Since Nikki told me she didn't need friends, I did not call her. However, a couple days later she called me. "Hey, Larry, you want to go to dinner again?" So we did, and, within a few weeks, we were constant companions. We ate meals together and went shopping or to the movies with each other. Oftentimes, we'd just listen to music or watch television at her apartment.

I ended up at places I hadn't been in years. Nikki would say, "Let's go shoot some pool." So we'd head for a pool table with me whispering a prayer of gratitude for my pool hall past. She got me out on the dance floor doing something else I hadn't done in a long time. I knew it was strange for a 47-year-old guy to be dancing with a college student, but we had fun together and we weren't concerned about what others were thinking.

We really enjoyed each other's company. Nothing physical ever went on between us yet there was a great emotional bond. Without Nikki realizing it, we were also developing a spiritual bond. I knew God had a purpose in our relationship.

One day after I started spending time with Nikki, my pastor, Dary Northrop, asked, "Larry, I know you've just come through the worst time of your life. How's it going these days, Man?"

"It's been tough, but I'm doing great," I told him. "God is fabulous."

"What are you doing with your time?"

"Well, since you're the most nonjudgmental, open-minded pastor I've ever met, I'll tell you," I answered. "My best friend is a stripper and I've been hanging out with her a lot."

Dary raised his eyebrows and leaned forward. "Wow! What's that all about?"

"All I can tell you is that God put us together. Nikki is a great Christian waiting to happen. I feel like that's what this is all about. It's good for both of us right now."

He took my hand and prayed with me. Then he said, "Larry, I'm glad I'm a happily married man and I can go home to my wife. I wouldn't trade places with you for anything. You be careful out there." And he sent me off with a high five. Dary was a mentor to me during that time and still is. I have a lot of respect and love for him.

As Nikki and I grew in our new friendship, the biblical mandate to be "in the world" but not "of the world" took on a whole new meaning for me. I found myself in situations I would have never imagined yet I was close to God, praying for guidance and protection. I never felt out of line.

God gave me a supernatural strength to keep up with Nikki. She would get off work at two in the morning, be home by three and call, wanting to go to breakfast. I got less sleep during that period of time than ever in my life yet had more energy. It was unbelievable.

One evening after we'd been hanging out together for close to a year, we were eating dinner in Old Town. It was a beautiful summer night; the sun was setting. We were relaxing on the patio, enjoying a great Italian meal, when Nikki surprised me by reaching across the table and putting her hand on mine.

"Larry," she said. "it happened. You've become the best friend I've ever had. Sometimes I can't believe you risked your reputation to hang out with a stripper like me. But you love me for who I am. You don't judge me for anything I do. You've never come on to me. You've never had an agenda with me. You just love me more than anybody else ever has in my life. Thank you."

I had been waiting for almost a year to share my faith with Nikki. The time had come. I said, "Nikki, I'm not the first guy who ever did anything like this."

"What do you mean?"

"Two thousand years ago," I said, "there was a man named Jesus . . ." And I told her the story from the Bible of the woman at the well and Jesus' love and kindness toward her.

Nikki was amazed. "That's in the Bible, Larry?"

"Yeah," I answered. "That's in the Bible and a lot of other great stories too."

"I want a Bible."

So I bought her one the next day, a little paperback student edition of the New International Version. At the front of the book, I wrote a note saying I hoped it would bring the joy to her life it had brought to mine.

When I gave it to Nikki she said, "I don't know how to start, where to start. The only experience I've had with religious things was when my grandmother used to take me to a Catholic church when I was a little girl."

"The first book of the New Testament," I told her, "the book of Matthew, ties in the Old Testament history with the New Testament times. It'll give you a good starting point. Now, when you read Matthew, some things are going to happen with you. Give me a call if you have any questions."

About nine o'clock that night the phone rang. It was Nikki. "You have to come over to my apartment right now!"

I hurried over to her place and found Nikki, the exotic dancer, adorned as always with extravagant makeup and jewelry, her hair piled high on her head, wearing short shorts. She was sitting Indian style on an ottoman with her little dog Snicker and her new Bible in her lap, each ankle accented by a dainty tattoo. I thought it was one of the most paradoxical pictures I had ever seen.

"There's a lot of stuff I have to ask you, Larry," she said. So we began talking about the Word of God. She couldn't get enough. We stayed up until 2:00 or 3:00 A.M. again, this time discussing Scripture. From that evening on, every night she didn't dance at the club, she studied the Bible. On those nights I studied with her. And I slept even less than before.

After a couple weeks of this, we went out one Saturday night to shoot some pool. In between games, Nikki asked, "Can I go to your mass with you tomorrow?"

"Sure, you can come to church with me anytime."

The next morning, I used the 15-minute drive between Nikki's place and the church to try to give her an idea of what to expect. "You know how we've been reading the New Testament?" I said. "Well, the way we worship at this church is very similar to the way they worshipped back then.

"Over the centuries, many big, formal churches have gotten into religious ruts and ritualistic patterns. Timberline Church just teaches the love of God. We get excited that God is changing our lives. We cheer at church the same way you cheer at Broncos games. We worship, we praise God; some people laugh, some people cry. We have a good time. I call it a *pep rally for life*."

It was summertime and Nikki, as usual, wasn't wearing much. Knowing we'd soon be at the church, I persuaded her to sit in the balcony with me, for two reasons besides her lack of clothing. One was so I could explain the service as it went on; the other was that the only woman my church had seen me with was my wife. I did not want to cause a commotion. Plus, if we sat down front, people might pay more attention to Noticeable Nikki than to the preacher.

After about two minutes in the balcony, she said, "I don't want to be way up here; I want to go down where I can see better." Since I knew there was no winning with Nikki, we headed for the front of the sanctuary. She plopped down Indian style on the first pew. The pastor caught my eye and smiled. He knew who she was.

From the moment of the first song there was an electricity in that sanctuary. Nikki pointed to her arm which had chill bumps all over it and asked, "What's up with that, Larry?"

I smiled. "That's the presence of the Spirit of the living God. You're going to feel it for the next hour."

She was mesmerized by the music. After the singing and worship time, Pastor Dary spoke. His theme was—*even though you've had walls built up your whole life, today they're coming down.* Nikki leaned over and whispered, "Did you call him last night?"

"Of course not," I replied. "We didn't get home until one in the morning."

"So how did he know that?" she demanded.

I murmured, "I'll explain later."

At the end of the service, Dary asked us all to stand. He said, "If you want to accept Jesus into your heart and have the walls come down in your life, put your hand up now."

I looked over at Nikki and there was this worldly-wise, tough little stripper with her hand in the air and tears running down her face. She made a commitment that morning which would change both our lives.

After Nikki became a believer in Jesus Christ, every time the church doors were open, we were there. And every night she wasn't working she read the Bible. God let me know it was His job, not mine, to tell her what she could do for a living, what she could or couldn't smoke and drink, what she should wear, and how she should talk. So I sat back and kept my mouth shut. I was an encouragement to her and she was an encouragement to me.

I watched Nikki begin to grow in her walk with the Lord. Two or three weeks after she became a believer, she called one night about 10:00 P.M. "Larry, you have to come over here right now," she said. "Something important has happened."

As usual, she was on the ottoman with Snicker and her Bible in her lap. "I just saw something incredible in the book of Matthew," she declared, tapping the Bible with her long red fingernail. "It says here He takes care of the lilies of the field and the birds of the air and He'll take even better care of me. This stuff is real. God promised it and He has to do it."

I nodded my head.

"You know what that told me tonight? It's wrong for me to take my clothes off for a living. It's wrong for me to make money that way. I have over $2,000 worth of bills per month and I pay those bills with my job. Without it, Larry, I could be very worried about paying my obligations, but God promised me in this Scripture I don't have to strip any more. Is that right or not?"

With a gulp and a prayer, I agreed.

Nikki never danced another striptease, and God kept His promise to provide for her. She became an integral part of our church. Teens gravitated toward her. They hung onto her every word. And Nikki didn't hold anything back with them.

"Look, you guys," she'd tell them, "some of you have been raised in strict homes. You might be looking forward to getting out and having the things of the world, like your own place, a nice car, parties, maybe even drinking and drugs, or times with the opposite sex. You think you want to go out and sow your wild oats. Well, I've been there; I've had it all. I've had *everything* the world has to offer and it can never begin to equal what Jesus has done in my life."

Nikki is a light to those around her and a continual inspiration to me. When I was down for the count, when I didn't know what God wanted to do with a used up 47-year-old, He, in His humorous and surprising way, showed me I was worth something to other people. He showed me, through my relationship with Nikki, that I was a valuable person, an important piece to the puzzle of her life by the power of His Spirit. God also showed me through her I had new chapters to write; I still had purpose in life.

My friendship with Nikki was the unexpected impetus for a unique outreach to single people that has blessed me with the most exciting, adventurous times of my life and also the most rewarding. I loved being married and I love being a parent; yet, befriending singles like Nikki in downtown Fort Collins has given me a sense of purpose and a thrill beyond anything I could have imagined.

I have introduced Nikki and many other young friends to their spouses-to-be as well as to the Lord; I've held their newborn babies; I've gotten to know their loved ones. We will be family and friends throughout the rest of this life and into eternity.

It's a God thing and it all started with that one little question, "Hey, you want to go out with me sometime?"

CHAPTER 5

CROWDED CAFES

I like to call Nikki "Little Simon Peter" because she reminds me of Jesus' most direct, most daring disciple. She's bold and more than ready and willing to tell people all about what Jesus has done in her life. One such incident happened not long after she became a Christian.

We had just sat down at a table in a restaurant when our mutual friend Lyndsey walked by. "Hi, guys," she smiled.

"Hey, Lyndsey," said Nikki, "you want to sit with us?"

Lyndsey sat down and we shared dinner and conversation. I'd always been impressed with Lyndsey, a cute college student as well as a dynamic, charismatic waitress who had often served us at another of our favorite restaurants. She had a great smile and a tremendous spirit that drew people to her.

We hadn't visited long when Lyndsey turned to Nikki. "I'm not usually this forward but I have to know. What in the world happened to you? I've never seen anybody change their look, their walk, their talk the way you have, Nikki. Something dramatic must have happened!"

Nikki got this big grin on her face, smiled at me, smiled at Lyndsey. Then she said, "Lyndsey, Jesus came into my life. I was an exotic dancer in Denver. I was wild. I was doing drugs. I was out of control. I was living right on the edge when Jesus came into my life. He totally changed me. Larry is my best friend and he introduced me to Jesus."

Lyndsey apparently hadn't expected that response. Tears welled in her eyes. She didn't know what to say. Finally, she leaned across the table and touched Nikki's arm. "I want what you have."

Nikki put her arm around my shoulder. "Larry, I got her this far. You're gonna have to take her the rest of the way!"

I asked Lyndsey, "When do you want to do this?"

"Now," she answered.

So I said, "We can take you down the street to my salon where we can have some privacy and talk to you about what it means to accept God into your heart and life."

"I know what it means," Lyndsey said. "It's something I was raised with but something I've gotten away from. I want God in my life."

So we walked down to the salon and back into a private room where we got down on our knees, hand-in-hand, as Lyndsey asked Jesus to come into her life. The next Sunday she sat on the second pew with me, watching Nikki sing in the choir. She and Nikki soon became close friends. Today, Lyndsey is one of the secretaries at Timberline Church and a vital part of the congregation.

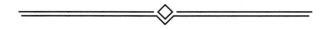

There were other instances of people recognizing something had happened in Nikki's life. One time a young lady named Samantha (name changed) from another salon called me up. She said, "Larry, you know Nikki, the stripper, who has Sharon do her nails? What in the world happened to her?"

I played dumb. "What do you mean?"

"Don't give me, 'What d'ya mean?' Something's happened to her. She doesn't walk the same, she doesn't talk the same, she doesn't dress the same, she doesn't act the same. She's a totally different person! What happened to her?"

"God came into her life," I answered, "and changed her into a new person."

Samantha was shocked. "Wow, that's amazing. When can I get with you two?"

We met that afternoon at a busy coffee shop down the street from my salon. As soon as we sat down Samantha turned to Nikki. "I want to know, out of your own mouth, what has happened to you."

Nikki smiled. "I'll just tell you what I've told a lot of other people. Jesus came into my life and completely changed me. I am a new person. The person you knew before was not who I was born to be. The person you're seeing now is who I was born to be."

Samantha said, "I want what you've got."

"That's great!" I interjected. "We'll get together tonight and talk about it."

"I want it now."

So Nikki pulled out her beat-up student NIV Bible, opened it up and explained to Samantha how to become a Christian. She told her God had a plan for each of us when He created us, but our sin keeps us from experiencing His plan. Because He loves us and wants His best for our lives, He sent His Son, Jesus, to save us from our sinful selves. All we have to do, she told Samantha, is accept the love and salvation He offers and His supernatural power to change us into new people.

"Do you believe this?" Nikki asked Samantha. "Do you want to ask Jesus into your heart?"

"Yes."

"Let's hold hands and pray," said Nikki. "You can do it right now." We all joined hands, bowed our heads and, right there in the middle of that crowded coffee shop, Samantha became a believer.

CHAPTER 6

A GOOD LIFE

Although it sounds incredible and much too coinciden-
tal, Nikki and Lyndsey married guys who had been
best friends since junior high. Matt and Mark played football and partied together in high school. After graduation,
they worked together at Coopersmith's, a large restaurant,
bar and poolroom in Old Town.

Matt was the manager at Coopersmith's and Mark was a
waiter there. Lyndsey waited tables for the restaurant next
door. One day Mark noticed her working the patio area
outside and it wasn't long before he asked her out.

Matt and Nikki, on the other hand, met inside
Coopersmith's a couple weeks after Nikki became a Christian.
We were shooting pool there one night when out of nowhere
she said, "Hey, you know the guy who runs this place—Matt,
I think his name is? He's cute."

Well, in all the time I'd been around Nikki, hardly any
guy ever turned her head. She was picky about who she
spent time with. When I heard her say, "That guy is really
cute. I think I might like to go out with him," I thought,
Whoa, I never heard you talk like that before.

"Why don't you go visit the ladies room," I said, "and
I'll have a little talk with him."

"You better not tell him I said I think he's cute!"

I laughed. "Of course I wouldn't say that."

She left and I went over to talk with Matt, a tall, serious, caring kind of guy who likes things orderly. All those characteristics made him a great manager. "Hey, Matt," I said, "you know my friend Nikki who comes in here with me all the time?"

"Yeah," he said. "I know who you mean. We call her the Avocado Queen."

I laughed. Everything Nikki ordered, even pizza, had avocados on it. "She'd probably shoot me if she knew I was telling you this, but you've kinda caught her eye. I know her well enough to believe that if you asked her out, she'd go."

"Really? You better not be putting me on, 'cause I don't want to ask somebody out and have them say 'no.'"

"I'm tellin' you, Man," I said, "she will."

About 15 minutes later, Matt walked by our pool table. I looked up. "Hey, Matt, I'd like to introduce you to my friend Nikki." Then I left to make a couple phone calls while they played a game of pool together.

Later on Nik told me what happened when Matt finally got up the courage to ask her out. My Little Simon Peter responded with, "I'll go out with you but you have to go to church with me first."

Here's this guy running a bar and she's telling him he has to go to church with her. Matt said, "I do, huh?"

She said, "Yeah, if you want to go out with me you gotta to go to church with me."

Sure enough, the next weekend Matt was in church with Nikki. It wasn't long before her faith became his faith too and they were on the road to a lifetime together.

After Lyndsey became a Christian, she grew concerned about Mark because he was not open spiritually. I was acquainted with Mark who is dark-haired, around six feet tall and someone who welcomes a good time. He is also a kind-hearted guy who enjoys helping people.

I had shot pool with Mark once or twice, but God prompted me to start spending more time with him. We played golf together, occasionally went out in the evening and eventually became really good buddies. I prayed for the time when I could talk with him about the Lord. One night I felt led to take him out to dinner. I knew it was time to discuss spiritual issues with Mark.

As we visited, he talked about the church service he had attended with Lyndsey. "The music is too intimate in that church," he told me. "It makes me uncomfortable. I don't like the feelings I get there. I wasn't raised in that kind of church and I don't see how I could go there regularly."

With a discouraged shrug he added, "I love Lyndsey, but I can't change who I am to be with her. I just don't know what's going to happen with us on this church thing."

It was a potential turning point in their relationship and I knew God had put me there to be a peacemaker. "Mark, you and I are good friends and we have a lot of respect for each other. I want to pass on a little wisdom to you.

"I know you love Lyndsey and you guys are planning on marrying. It's going to be increasingly important as time goes on for you two to go to the same church, to have the same belief system, and for your children to share those beliefs. Any book, any counselor will tell you what I'm telling you. It's incredibly important. You can't have a completely fulfilled marriage without the spiritual part.

"You've told me you would like to go to a church with Lyndsey but not that church. I admire you for your candor and I think there's a way you might handle this gracefully. I'd like to offer you a suggestion, if you're interested."

Mark nodded, but by the doubtful look on his face, I figured he was thinking something like, *Oh yeah, what?*

Hurriedly I continued. "Go to Lyndsey and say, 'Lyndsey, I am willing to attend your church for the next six weeks. If I don't like it at the end of six weeks and know I can never stomach it, I'd like you to go to a church of my choosing with me for six weeks. Then we'll make a decision.'" To my relief, Mark relaxed and agreed to try my idea.

In the following weeks Mark and I shot pool, played golf and got together for lunch. Finally, one day he said, "You know, Larry, that church isn't so bad. The pastor is a really good speaker. I'm getting to where I don't dislike it as much as I used to."

Well, as you can probably guess, when the six weeks were finished, he liked Timberline Church. In fact, Mark became a Christian, he and Lyndsey were married, and they have been happily attending church together ever since. They are also now proud parents of two sweet little girls.

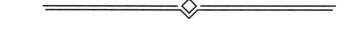

Not long after Mark and Lyndsey's marriage, I received a phone call from Nikki in Iowa where she and Matt had moved. She called to ask us to pray for Matt who was in a lot of pain. The doctors had just found cancer throughout his abdomen. Emergency surgery was expected within 24 hours.

When Nikki called about Matt's illness, Lyndsey, Mark and I dropped everything, hopped in a car and drove to Iowa. We arrived about two hours before the surgery. You could have cut the dread in that hospital room with a knife. It was a heavy thing for a 25-year-old to face.

I took Nikki off to the side. "The doctor says Matt is full of cancer," she cried. I comforted her as best I could, then the five of us prayed together. It was an emotional time, a time of human fear of the unknown. Yet, we felt the supernatural peace only God can give.

After they rolled Matt away to surgery, Nikki collapsed in my arms. "Larry," she whispered, "why is God letting this happen to us? I've been obedient. I've put Him first in my life. What could this possibly be about? I prayed with all my heart and you've told me I have a strong gift of faith. Why hasn't God healed Matt?"

I am rarely at a loss for words, but I didn't have an answer for Nikki. Instead, I hugged her as tight as I could. Then, my voice cracking, I said, "I don't know what the outcome of this will be, but you're holding a living, walking miracle, someone who has seen the power of God deliver him from the depths. I can't promise you a miracle for Matt, but I can promise you that, no matter what happens in this hospital, God *will* give you a good life. That's all I can promise you."

The seven hours of surgery were the longest any of us had ever experienced. When the doctor finished he came to talk with us. "Well," he said with a weary, sad shake of his head, "we opened him up. One of his kidneys was full of the tumor so we had to take it out. The growth had spread everywhere. We took lymph nodes and every bit of tumor we could find throughout his abdominal cavity.

"But we don't know if we got it all. This is a cancer research hospital and it looks like a worst case scenario to us. We sewed him back up and all we can do now is watch for the test results."

Two days later, after a lot of waiting and prayer, the report came back. "We don't understand why," we were told, "but it's not cancer. It is not malignant. Matt should recover." Shouting and laughing with joy, we all praised the Lord and returned home with a renewed faith in an incredible God.

Matt went on to become a policeman, something not normally possible with only one kidney. He even scored first in the physical fitness portion of the police academy testing and is now an up-and-comer in the Des Moines Police Department.

CHAPTER 7

THE BEAT

Being obedient to the Lord gives me a passion for living and a sense of excitement because I never know what's around the next corner. When I stopped trying to do everything my own way and in my own time, a freedom came to live moment by moment and to expect adventure. That's one of the greatest thrills of being a Christian, something I'd missed for years.

As a result of this adventure I'm on, I've met a lot of interesting people and have actually had men say to me, "Wow, you're always with the coolest women. When I get to be your age I want to be just like you. What's your secret?" They think I have some Viagra-type magic formula they can use, too.

My response is to put my arm around the guys, smile and say, "All I do is love these people more than they've ever been loved before. I really care about them." They usually raise their eyebrows, shrug and turn back to the pool table.

One of those "cool women" was a young lady I met while walking downtown named Lisa. Over time, my morning prayer walks had evolved into an enjoyable habit of strolling around Old Town between haircuts. I walked not only for the enjoyment but because I was grateful I could walk.

Soon I realized my daily hikes were a good way to keep in contact with others who, like Lisa, work downtown. Eventually, I developed a several-times-a-day routine which includes friendships as well as exercise. And, somewhere along the line, I started calling that routine "my beat."

Lisa worked at a unique Old Town clothing store called The Wildflower. She was also a Colorado State University student from an affluent family, drove a new car, and was the picture of togetherness. With her long, blond hair and blue eyes, she looked like she should be playing volleyball on a sun-drenched California beach with a bunch of buff, bronze, young guys. Despite her beach girl appearance, however, Lisa was bashful and reserved.

Not long after I met Lisa, she came in for a haircut. When I finished, she smiled shyly and asked, "You seem like a fun guy. Would you like to hang out some night?"

I said, "Sure, whenever you want."

"Why don't you pick me up at the store next Thursday after work." Lisa worked about a block away, so on Thursday night I walked over to get her and we ended up at the Rio. We were making the usual small talk at the restaurant when all of a sudden she opened up and started telling me about herself.

After about 15 minutes of talking, she exclaimed, "I can't believe I'm telling a total stranger these things. I'm normally a shy person and here I am telling you everything."

"It's OK," I said. "We're having a great time. If you're comfortable talking about yourself, I'm comfortable listening. I can tell we're going to be good buds."

So she continued. Occasionally, as Lisa talked, guys her age would stop at our table and ask, "Hey, Lisa, you want to go out dancing tonight?"

"Maybe later," she'd say. "I'm talking to my friend Larry right now."

After we'd visited awhile she asked, "You want to go dancing?"

I gave my standard answer, "Sure, why not." I've come to realize in this new lifestyle that you can be out rubbing shoulders with "the world," as the Bible calls it, whether on a dance floor or in a nightclub, restaurant or a movie theater, yet not be a part of that world. The biblical directive to be in the world but not of the world is not necessarily referring to where we are, what we're doing, who we're with or the way we're dressed, but what our agenda is.

I can be on the dance floor enjoying a good time with a good friend, laughing, blowing off steam and getting exercise, yet embrace a totally different agenda than the couple next to us trying to hook up for the night. I thank God for the opportunity to have fun with other singles.

So we went dancing. I had to go home first to change clothes because I knew I needed to wear "grunge" where we were going. When I met Lisa at the nightclub, she said, "Wow, you even know what to wear. That's cool." We had a great time that night.

About a week passed, then Lisa called. "You want to go out Thursday night?"

Again, we ended up at the Rio. We hadn't even sat down when she said, "Larry, I have to talk to you about something." She seemed very serious. "I just want to tell you there's something about you that's different from anybody I've ever met. I don't know how to describe it. You're like the dad I was never close to, the big brother I never had, and the best friend I always wanted, all wrapped up into one person."

With a bashful grin, she added, "I guess you symbolize to me what a man is supposed to represent to a woman.

I don't understand it but I really love it and I love hanging out with you."

I hugged her, tears in my eyes. "That's the nicest compliment I've ever received."

I didn't see Lisa for a couple weeks. And then, one Saturday evening she called me from her home. "I don't feel like going out tonight. Would you come over to the house? I really need to talk to you about something."

I drove to the place she shared with three other college roommates. They were in the kitchen so we had some privacy, with Lisa's dog, Tucker, in the living room. "Pull up a chair," Lisa said. "I have something I need to discuss."

"What's on your mind?" I asked as I sat down.

"I want to know what your secret is," she said. "You've been through a lot of tragedy and yet you have fun in life, you love people. You don't hang onto regrets, you don't have bitterness; you just really love to live life and I want to be able to do that, too. I want to know your secret."

I like to be cautious when people begin to open up their hearts to the Lord. I don't want to be heavy handed and drive them away. Knowing Lisa was a university student immersed in a humanistic environment, I wanted to walk carefully. "Lisa," I said, "this has to do with my faith in God. Do you want to talk about that?"

"Yes," she said. "I want to hear it."

"Do you want to hear the whole thing?" I asked. "This could take an hour or two."

"Yes."

So I talked about how in our culture the "creature," mankind, has become bigger in our eyes than our Creator—God. People don't like to recognize there's a supernatural power who not only created them but can change their lives. Because we're programmed that way since childhood, it's hard for those from our culture and educational system to open up to God. It seems illogical to us.

I told Lisa how I was a skeptic about religious things during my rebellious youth. And I told her stories of the miracles God had performed for me since those days. She listened intently for over an hour. In conclusion, I said, "Lisa, when you go back to class on Monday, chances are this conversation will seem far away, like a dream. Do you want this to be a reality in your life?"

She responded, "Yes."

"Let me pray with you that God will make these truths imminent in your mind and that you'll have a desire to deal with what I've shared with you; that it will become a reality in your heart and life. And, when you're ready to accept the Lord into your life, I'll be there for you."

The next week she called asking, "Can I go to your church with you?"

As we sat down in the pew Sunday morning, the worship team began to play and tears started streaming down Lisa's face. They weren't tears of regret or sorrow or guilt; they were tears of peace. Lisa looked like she was finally home.

Like always, we heard a tremendous message from Dary. When he finished, he asked if anybody wanted to accept the Lord. Lisa raised her hand immediately. Then the tears rolled down my face, too. After church we went out for a celebration lunch. Lisa told me she felt wonderful.

The next morning I was eating breakfast at a restaurant when my pager vibrated. So I found a pay phone and returned a call from Lisa.

"Larry," she said with a happy voice, "you don't know what happened to me in church yesterday."

"Sure I do. The Lord came into your heart."

"That's true, but there's a lot more you don't know about me. I know it looks like I have it all together, yet I've practically been an alcoholic for over a year. I've had wrong relationships with several guys and gotten hurt many times. I've had really low self-esteem for as far back as I can remember. And

I've had health problems related to my emotional problems just as long. But all that changed yesterday.

"I talked with my mom last night and told her, 'You know how I've been going to that counselor all these years, Mom? How you and Dad have spent so much money on me, but things haven't gotten any better? Well, I went to church with Larry yesterday and God came into my life. I'm changed. I feel like we can drop the counselor right now. I know I'm going to be OK.'"

That was three years ago and Lisa's life has truly been changed. Just before she moved away awhile back, we went to church together. Sitting next to her, I thought about what God had done in her life and thanked Him I had been able to be a part of it.

The words of a note Lisa sent me early in our friendship show how God used Christian companionship in her life:

Dear Larry,

You've helped me a lot lately and I don't know how to thank you for lifting my spirits. You are an unbelievable person who I envy through my weak eyes. I know down deep inside I too can have the energy and hope you carry with you each step in your life. I must have patience and strength but I am going to latch onto that spirit one way or another.

Sometimes when I look at life, I don't get the meaning or purpose but when I hear you talk and see the way you are and the way you think, I understand the love you have for life. Your friendship means an awful lot to me. I hope you realize that.

Larry, I hope you can help turn my life into what it's meant to be. I know I can't do it alone, but who can? Right now, I've been so up and down and I know I can't continue to live in this way. Thank you. You are a true friend and I'm so happy to have met you. I love you. Thanks for all your smiles and hope in me.

Love, Lisa

CHAPTER 8

I'LL SEE YOU AGAIN

Although being single isn't always easy, especially since I enjoy marriage, God has given me a great life. He has blessed me with an abundance of good friends and good times. The Lord not only sends men and women for me to minister to, He sends friends to minister to me. They keep me from suffering the devastating loneliness singles often feel. And they help fill my cup so I can give to others.

One of those encouragers was Jami, a gorgeous, green-eyed blonde introduced to me in 1994 by a friend who said, "You both have lots of energy and a zest for living. So I thought you two should meet." He was right. Jami and I did have much in common and found we could talk with each other for hours.

Not long after we met, one evening at dinner Jami said, "Larry, I think we're going to be good friends and we're going to be spending quite a bit of time together. But there's something I have to tell you before our friendship goes any further. You need to know God has first place in my life because He has miraculously changed me. I'd like to tell you about it."

I nodded my head. "I'd like to hear about it."

"I used to be a party girl," Jami continued. "When I lived in Denver I dated several of the Broncos and met a lot of people in the fast lane. I drank a lot; partied hard. It probably won't surprise you that my wild, fast paced lifestyle did not include God.

"Never in my life did I consider having a relationship with Him. It just wasn't something I had ever heard or thought about." She shook her blonde hair as though amazed by her own ignorance. "Yet, one night while I was taking a shower, a Presence came into the bathroom and a Voice came into my mind saying, 'Jami, the life you're living is not what I want for you. I'm your Creator; I'm your God. I have a purpose for you and it's not what's going on with your life right now.'

"Shocked, I dropped to my knees right there in the shower, the water still running, and gave my life to God. He made me into a new person. And, because God is now first in my life, I have made a commitment to Him that I won't be physically involved with anyone until I get married." Jami smiled at me. "I like to tell this to guys I spend a lot of time with because I want them to know my beliefs up front."

I took her hand and squeezed it. "You're talking to the right guy, Jami. God is also first in my life and I, too, plan to not be physically involved with anyone unless I'm married to her. I'm so glad you shared your story and your feelings with me. Isn't God good to put two such like-minded people together!"

That was one of many great evenings with Jami. We had a lot of friends in common and a lot of fun around town. We went to movies, shot pool, had dinner or just talked almost every night. We discussed the joys of winning other people to the Lord and what He had done in our lives, how He was leading us. We also laughed a lot. Jami made you laugh about everything. She laughed at herself and she made me laugh at myself.

After we'd been hanging out together for several months, we were invited to the wedding of a friend. We usually took Jami's car when we went places together since she had a nice car and I didn't. Plus, she said she wasn't a good driver, so I always drove.

That particular night, however, we took separate cars because she had a get-together with her family after the reception. We stayed until 9:30 or 10:00 P.M. when Jami hurriedly left, rushing to be with her family. I drove to my apartment and went to bed.

But, I was awakened at 3:30 A.M. by the telephone ringing. Her voice trembling, one of Jami's friends cried, "Jami had a terrible car accident! She's in the hospital with a broken neck." The young woman choked back a sob. "She's . . . she's paralyzed from the neck down and close to death."

That dark night and the dreadful drive to the hospital is forever imprinted on my memory. In my groggy state, I felt like I was in the middle of a bizarre nightmare. I so badly did not want to believe Jami was severely injured.

The sign on the door of the intensive care unit said, "Family Members Only." However, though I'd never met them, Jami's parents had left word for the nurses to let me in. I tiptoed inside and there lay Jami, her face bruised and swollen, her hair matted with blood and her body hooked up to every possible modern medical machine.

As I stood staring at her in shock and disbelief, tears running down my face, not knowing what to do or say, Jami opened her big, beautiful eyes and said, "Hey, Lar, how you doin', Buddy?" I didn't even have a chance to ask how she was feeling before she asked about me.

I carefully took her hand and we talked and cried together about her situation. She told me, "I've always known God put you in my life for a reason, Larry, but I didn't know why. Now, I think it's because of your paralysis experience a few years ago and the way God brought you through that. You'll be able to help me keep focused on Him."

When I returned the next day, she had a big smile on her face. "Larry, I'm going to make you go to work every day, even though you don't want to. The waiting room—we'll call it the condo—is right down the hall and has a couch that makes into a bed. You go to work every day, then come be with me every night and we'll make it through this thing together."

Jami had the most astonishing attitude which could have only come from God. She was not in denial; she knew exactly what was going on. She understood her circumstances and yet kept that "peace which passes all understanding" as well as her sense of humor. Her personality never diminished. If anything, Jami was more personable than ever.

One night after I finished feeding her, I pushed the tray away and got down just a few inches from her face. As I brushed the hair off her forehead, Jami asked, "Could you scratch my eyelid?" So I did that for her. We were inches apart and I sensed our feelings for each other had intensified since the accident.

Gazing into her green eyes, I couldn't help but say, "Jami, you are the most incredible woman, in every way, in *every* way."

She responded, "No, Larry, not in every way. I'm a terrible driver." She really caught me off guard, and we laughed and laughed.

The entire hospital staff knew about Jami. Doctors from other wards stopped in to see her. Nurses from all over the hospital visited that remarkable, spirited woman. For me, every night was an emotional combination of sorrow, joy, and a sense of privilege, being that special person for her at a crisis time in her life.

On my way from the "condo" to work Friday morning, I stopped to see Jami. "Listen, young man," she grinned, "tonight is Friday night and it's date night. I expect you to be here, dressed up, with flowers in your hand, Buddy, 'cause we're gonna have a date tonight!"

I walked in that evening as she had instructed me, wearing a sport coat and carrying flowers. The look on her face was priceless. "You didn't forget!"

Then she said, "It is date night, but we're going to share our date because some good friends have come to town. I've decided we're going to have a party."

We rounded up all the food we could get our hands on in that hospital. We fed it to Jami, we ate it ourselves, and we had a good time. Jami was the life of the party. She told jokes, she made us laugh, and she made us all so glad we were there.

It was an amazing evening but the most remarkable moment was when Jami said, "We've had a wonderful time together tonight. I feel like we should all join hands to say a prayer of thanks to God for His goodness."

After we'd formed a circle around her bed, she said, "Larry, you know I've never prayed aloud in front of you before—I'm kind of shy about that—but tonight I want to pray."

I smiled at her, nodded and she closed her eyes.

"Dear God," Jami prayed, "I just want to thank you for all your blessings in my life. I don't deserve the love and friendship I've been given this week. Thank you for letting me live this week. I don't come asking you for anything except to bless my friends. I want to thank you again for all you've done for me. Amen." To this day, I feel like that was the most fantastic prayer I've ever heard.

Saturday night, Jami's health took a turn for the worse. When I stopped by after church on Sunday, the head of neurosurgery told me, "Larry, I've got some bad news. Jami is having a rough time. In rare cases, paralysis goes up the spinal column and this is one of those cases. Jami is no longer able to breathe on her own. On top of that, she's having problems with her heart and other organs. This looks very serious."

The medical staff and her family were with her a lot on Sunday, so I didn't get to spend any time with Jami. Monday, my heart was heavy all day and I prayed constantly for Jami.

When I walked into intensive care that evening, her father met me, his eyes sad and serious. "The doctors have decided to do emergency surgery on Jami's stomach and some other organs. There's a lot of swelling. This is basically life or death surgery.

"I think you should go see her now," he said as he squeezed my shoulder. "They're taking her into surgery in just a few minutes."

I dreaded seeing Jami in that awful condition yet I realized I needed to be there for her. She was wide awake when I walked in. The doctors had told her what was going on, so she was aware of the gravity of her situation. I got as close to her as I could and put my hand on her face. "Jami," I said, "I love you with all my heart."

The only physical freedom Jami had had in the last week was the ability to talk. Now that function had left her also. She mouthed the words back to me, "I love you, too."

I looked in her eyes and saw uncertainty, pain, gladness I was there, and the most graphic picture of peace I've ever seen. "Jami, you know I'm not just saying this. If I could, I would trade places with you."

She mouthed the words, "I know you would."

Again I said, "I love you."

"I love you, too."

"I'll see you again."

She formed the words, "I'll see you again." Then they wheeled her out of the room.

Jami died in surgery and I did not see her again. Yet, I know without a doubt we'll have a wonderful reunion in heaven someday.

Some of my friends have said, "Wow, you finally met somebody special and then she died."

I don't look at it that way. It was a joy to know Jami and a privilege to be there for her during her last days on earth. I still keep a picture of her on my desk at the salon so I can be reminded of her love for God and her love of life. I have no regrets, only gladness because I was fortunate enough to be a part of her life for that short time.

During her nine-day ordeal, I told Jami, "Because of your extraordinary display of faith in this situation, you're going to affect a lot of people spiritually."

In all sincerity, Jami responded, "Larry, if one of our friends or family members comes to the Lord through this, it's worth it."

Jami's mother has since told me she became a believer because of her daughter's unflinching faith. Others have also been deeply affected by Jami's life and death.

There were over 400 people at her funeral. Jami was an unforgettable woman who continues to be an inspiration to everyone who knew her. People still talk about how much fun she was and what a strong faith she had. Years later, it's not unusual for someone to say, "Wasn't that Jami somethin' else!"

CHAPTER 9

THE NEXT LEVEL

Since God started connecting me with other singles, I have been more aware of His voice. I don't actually hear an audible voice but I have an impression or a feeling I should do something. For instance, one evening after Saturday night church I felt like I should go walk my downtown beat.

That night as I strolled through the Rio, an acquaintance named Heidi waved me over. "Sit down with us for a moment, Larry," she said. So I sat down and she introduced me to her companion, Marie. Heidi and Marie were both in their late 20s and quite a contrast in appearance. Heidi is an attractive, blue-eyed blonde from a staunch German family; Marie is Hispanic and Italian, very exotic looking.

"Marie has been my best friend since junior high," said Heidi. "She just moved here from Greeley and she's a terrific hair stylist. Do you have any openings at your place?"

"Interestingly enough," I responded, "we had someone leave a couple weeks ago, moved out of state. So I do have an opening in the salon right now."

"Can you interview me?" Marie asked. "Or can I fill out an application on Monday?"

I've had five salons and hired over 100 people during the 20 years I've been in Fort Collins. I like to give people a chance without going through all the applications and resumes. God helps me discern who to hire and who not to hire. So I said, "Nah, you're hired." She was amazed. Later that night we all went out dancing; had some great laughs and a good time together.

On Monday morning, Marie brought in her tools and set up her work station. During the weekend she had recruited some clients so started right in. I peeked over the divider and saw that she was one of the most talented hair stylists I'd ever met. I was very pleased, not only with the work she did, but also with her personality and her enthusiasm. *This is going to be great for both of us*, I thought.

When we each had a break in our appointments, I said, "Let's go up to the corner and I'll buy you a cup of coffee." After we sat down I told her, "You do fabulous work, Marie."

"Thanks a lot, Larry," she responded. "I really appreciate that. And I'm glad to be working in your salon." While we were basking in that happy moment, tears suddenly filled Marie's eyes. She looked down.

"I don't know why I'm telling you this, but I need to get it off my conscience." Marie's voice began to quiver. "Larry, I can't believe you hired me without checking my background. I've been a crack addict for years."

She looked up at me. "In fact, I just got out of jail last week and moved here to make a new start. If you had checked out my past you might not have hired me. Thank you so much for giving me a job."

Surprised by the outburst, I just nodded. She continued, "I accepted God into my life several months ago and He is changing me. With His help I'm going to get over this addiction." Marie wiped at her tears. "I haven't had any drugs since I got saved. Thank you, Larry, for helping me make a new start in Fort Collins."

I took her hand. "Marie, God has dropped you right where He wants you. Of all the places you could have worked, God brought you to this salon. He wants you here because I love the Lord and I try to put Him first in my life. I plan on being your best friend and your spiritual mentor, if you want me to be."

The next morning we returned to the same shop for coffee again. As we shared the good things going on in our lives, how great God is, what He was doing, Marie reached across the table, took my hand and said, "Thank you again, Larry . . ." Her voice trailed off as she looked up, a surprised expression on her face.

I turned around. Towering above me was an immense black man, six feet and 220 pounds of solid muscle. His angry eyes were riveted on me.

"Oh, uhm . . . Larry," said Marie, "I want you to meet my husband, Lee. We're in the process of a divorce right now."

Since I started hanging out with the downtown crowd, I've occasionally been in situations where I wanted to run. This was certainly one of them, even though we weren't doing anything wrong. In fact, we were doing a good thing, praising God. But Lee didn't look like he shared our enthusiasm.

Marie asked him to sit down. Lee slowly lowered his massive frame next to her petite one, his dark eyes continuing to bore holes through me. Marie looked from him to me and started blurting out things about their marriage problems I couldn't believe.

Then, still holding my hand, she turned to her husband. "Lee, God has sent this man into my life to be my best friend, to help me get over my addictive patterns, including the addictive pattern you and I have had in our marriage. If we are ever to be together again as man and wife, I have to be healed and you have to be healed; God has to be first in our home. He has put Larry in our lives to help us. I just met him last weekend but I truly love him."

Her hot hand on mine felt like a pulsating neon sign flashing, *Sic 'em, sic 'em, sic 'em!* Lee looked like he got the message loud and clear and was about to reach his brawny biceps across the table to wring my neck. I quickly scanned the room wondering, *How fast can I get out of here if I need to?*

Suddenly, Lee held out his huge hand. Seeing tears in his eyes and the smile on Marie's face, I cautiously offered mine for a handshake.

"It's true, Larry," he said, crushing my hand in his. "Everything Marie said is true, and I know it. God is speaking to me right now as we sit here. I believe He has placed you in our lives for this purpose."

That night Lee and I went to dinner together and had a great talk about what God wanted in his and Marie's lives. I discovered Lee is friendly, charming, and also a hair stylist. In fact, he's one of the top stylists in northern Colorado.

Because of Marie's problems, they both agreed she needed to make a new start in Fort Collins at that stage of her life. Lee was troubled by some lifestyle problems of his own and would remain in Greeley, about a half-hour away. Their young daughter Janez would live with Marie's sister as long as necessary.

Lee and Marie had hearts for God, but they were each struggling with addictions. A long, long road lay ahead for them, their marriage, and their family.

Marie was one of those special people God placed in my life, not only for me to help her, but also for her to help me by being a close friend. She's a sweet, generous, kind-spirited person who likes to laugh and loves to please others. As the months progressed, her business thrived and we enjoyed each other's company. Almost every Saturday night we went to church together.

I learned Marie had endured severe abuse in her childhood. Her family was as dysfunctional as they come. That background led to many of her addictive qualities. Despite all that's happened to her, however, Marie is known for her great smile and big heart.

Sometimes when I was with Marie, I could see a faraway look in her eyes. I knew she was longing to have her family back together, to be with Janez and Lee, to be a happy, whole, healthy person. Yet, since I had never struggled with addictions, it was hard for me to understand what she was going through.

I remember one night when she was feeling down, I said something like, "Wow, it's so devastating the way drugs tear up families and destroy self-esteem. You just have to wonder, why would a person do that to themselves?"

Marie grabbed my shoulders. "Larry," she cried, tears streaming down her face, "do you think I *want* to be addicted?"

Her reaction changed the way I look at dependencies. Those who are addicted are sick people who need help and supernatural healing. Marie's addiction was way beyond anything I could handle or understand. It was something only God could heal. I gained a compassion that night for drug and alcohol addicts I hadn't had before.

One night when we were out together at the Rio, we ran into some mutual friends of Marie's and Lee's. The friends began talking about Lee's activities, the people he was running with, negative things he was doing. I saw a look flash across Marie's face I hadn't seen before, a desperate look. A few minutes later, she excused herself saying, "I have something I have to do."

Early the next morning I received a phone call from Marie. She had driven to Greeley the night before, gotten into a heated discussion with Lee, lost control and done crack again. She ended up hospitalized with policemen guarding her. She was allowed only one phone call, so she called me.

"Please come and get me," Marie begged. "They've given me two choices. I have to either go back to jail or to a rehab center in Santa Fe, New Mexico. You can tell them how I'm trying to change, Larry."

The severity of Marie's situation hit me full force. I didn't know what to do. She was sobbing and pleading, "Larry, please, please come and get me. You can explain everything. You can talk to them. You can make it OK."

But God seemed to be saying to me, *No, you cannot rescue Marie from this. All you can do is be her best friend and turn the rest over to me.*

"If you don't come in the next 45 minutes," Marie cried, "they're going to take me away!"

"I love you, Marie," I said, "and I'm going to pray about this."

She wept. "Please, Larry, please come and get me."

"We have to do what's right," I said. Then I hung up the telephone.

I really struggled that night because I wanted so badly to jump in the car and rescue Marie, but I knew her problems were bigger than any help I could offer, and I knew I would have to let her go to the rehab center. Though I felt that was what God wanted for Marie, I tossed and turned and prayed all night.

The rehabilitation program was long and severe, almost like a boot camp. Marie could not have contact with her friends. She could only speak with her mother once a month by telephone for a short while. And she could only talk to her daughter once every two or three months.

Losing Marie left a big hole in my heart and my life. I prayed for her every day but I missed the messages she used to leave on my voice mail. "Larry, you're my best friend," she'd say. "I love you. Thanks for helping me with God." I missed her but I knew only God could take her to the next level.

Thirteen months later Marie finally called again. "Larry, I'm home! And I'm so glad to hear your voice! Come and see me."

I drove to Greeley as quickly as I could and met her at a restaurant where we hugged and cried. "Larry," she said, "that was hell on earth! I was mad at you for awhile for not rescuing me but I now know why you did what you did.

"I was allowed two pictures in my room," she continued. "So I put up one of Lee and Janez and the other was of you. You've been my best friend the last two years. I prayed every night, 'Let me see my friends again. Let me be with my family. Let me have the kind of life You want me to have.'"

We had a great talk that night. Both of us knew she'd come a long way but still had a long way to go. We also knew that, with God's help, she could make it through the tough times.

Marie had no home and no transportation, so she moved in with her parents, which is a tough thing to do when you're 30 years old and from a dysfunctional family. She found a job in a salon a couple miles from her folks' house and walked to and from work every day.

I drove over twice a week to have dinner with her. Life was difficult, but I promised her she was going to be the greatest version of Marie she had ever been. She was going to make it this time.

"For the first time in my life," Marie told me, "I've forgiven myself. I can even say I love myself now. I've hated myself my whole life and that's where my problems have come from. But I know I'm going to have a good life again. I know God has brought me this far for a purpose."

"Because you keep taking more and more healing steps," I said, "I can see you someday standing in front of hundreds of people saying, 'If I can recover from being a crack addict, which they say is incurable, and if God can restore me to the woman I am now, He can do it for you, too.'

"I know God has a plan and a purpose for your life a lot bigger than you've ever imagined. You just have to keep taking the right steps now."

One night Marie said, "Larry, as much as I love and appreciate my mom and dad, it's really hard for me to be in the house where I grew up. And it's hard to walk to work and not have anything at all.

"I'm not complaining. These are just feelings I have while I'm struggling to get back on my feet, as I'm working on becoming the person God wants me to be. These are the realities. I sure wish I could live somewhere else, but I don't have the money for an apartment."

Then she asked, "Will you pray with me about a place to live?" We knelt down beside my car and prayed, "God, would you give Marie encouragement about her living arrangements and show her things are going to get better in a concrete kind of way? We know you're a God of miracles because we've seen your power in both our lives."

The next afternoon Marie called, a lilt in her voice. "Larry, the most amazing thing just happened! An old friend I haven't seen in years stopped by, this Christian girl I used to work with named Tammy.

"She said to me, 'Marie, for some reason you've really been on my heart and mind lately and I had to come see you today. I don't know what your living arrangements are now but I'm asking you to live with me if you'd like. I have a good-sized house with plenty of room for both of us.'" That was a direct answer to our prayer of the night before and it was tremendously uplifting to Marie.

Marie is still in counseling and working toward full recovery. In the meantime, her business has prospered and her family is back together. She and Lee and Janez are all living in the same house, united again, this time as a Christ-centered family.

"The things I have now are the things I've wanted my whole life," says Marie. "I've always wanted to be in a good marriage, to make a home for my husband and my daughter, and, since becoming a Christian, to be serving the Lord together with Lee. Despite all I've been through, nobody in the world could be happier than I am."

Lee has shared with me the struggle he had when Marie came back from the rehab program. He was afraid to take a chance with her again. Plus, his family insisted he not renew the relationship. Yet, something told him, "She's really changed this time."

Lee, who is also making good progress with his own addictions, says, "I thank God every day for my family." With a smile, he adds, "When I look at the three of us together, I know I'm seeing a modern-day miracle. And that really makes me happy."

CHAPTER 10

HEIDI THE ATHEIST

Marie's friend Heidi, being a logical, prove-it-to-me type of person, was known as "Heidi the Atheist" in high school. When Marie began to change, Heidi just sat on the sidelines observing, very skeptical that Marie could get off drugs. She was also suspicious of anything that had to do with Jesus, a Creator God or any traditional religious concept. Yet, she began to see things happening in Marie's life which were hard to explain logically.

I was also the object of Heidi's scrutiny. She searched for a chink in my armor, watching to see if I would make a pass at her or any of her friends. She could tell I was a normal, red-blooded male who was naturally attracted to the opposite sex. So it impressed Heidi to see that, through the discipline God gave me, I was able to behave the right way with women. It was important to her that my walk matched my talk.

Heidi asked me questions to try to stump me or side-track me about my beliefs. I explained my beliefs in the way God's Spirit has shown me, telling her Jesus was not a religious man and Christianity is not about jumping through religious hoops; it's about unconditional love. Then she began to see Christianity demonstrated in Marie's life and my life and through church friends who reached out to Marie.

At one point in our growing friendship, I felt led to give Heidi a book called *More Than A Carpenter* by Josh McDowell which is based on facts and logic about Jesus' life. I wrote in the front something like:

> I am giving this to you because you are a truth seeker and you like to deal in reality and facts—that's what this book is about. I pray you will come to experience the joy I have had in my life since I opened myself up intellectually and spiritually to the truth of the Gospel. I think you can find truth between these pages.
>
> This is a gift. I don't expect a response. Read it at your own pace and in your own time. I don't ever expect anything back from you or for you to even say you read it. I just give it as a gift to you.

About two months later, one of Heidi's friends came in for a haircut. "You will never believe what happened this weekend!" she exclaimed. "Heidi the Atheist came to my church last Sunday and accepted Jesus as her Savior!"

"Hey, that's great news!" I said.

Then she added, "When we went out for lunch afterwards, she told me about a book you gave her that made her want to open up to the possibility of believing in God."

The friend laughed as she related the story. "You know what Heidi said when I asked her if I could borrow that book?"

"No. What?"

"She said, 'Well, I guess so. But, Larry gave it to me, so you'd better read it fast and give it back right away!'"

Heidi and Marie are closer than ever now that God is in both of their lives. Nobody could be happier for Marie and her new lifestyle than her best friend Heidi who didn't believe Marie could ever get off drugs.

CHAPTER 11

ONE-MAN ISLAND

Over the years, I have developed a regular clientele in my hair styling business. As a result of seeing my clients every four to six weeks, I learn a lot about their lives and families. Oftentimes, we become good friends. But, for some reason, that didn't happen with Bill. He remained a casual acquaintance though I'd cut his hair for eight or nine years.

In his mid-30s, Bill is tall, dark, handsome and graying at the temples. He wears expensive, tailored suits with highly polished shoes and always looks the part of the successful businessman that he is. During haircuts, we talked about golf and travel and briefly touched on relationships but never had a real in-depth friendship, though we attended the same church.

Bill's introduction to Timberline Church came through Nikki's baptism. Following her conversion, Nikki took a course in nail care and began doing nails at my salon. When she decided to get baptized, she insisted everyone who worked with her attend her baptism. Nikki wouldn't take "no" for an answer.

One of the ladies who went, Marilyn, was really touched by the service and began attending our church regularly. Eventually, she became a strong believer and started sharing her faith and asking people to go to church with her. Bill was one of those who visited Timberline with Marilyn.

Several months later, I was out on the golf course one morning when I felt my pager vibrate. I looked at the readout and was surprised to see the call was from Bill. After I finished my round of golf, I found a phone and listened to his message. Bill is a former professional baseball player, a big, strong guy not given to outward signs of emotion—but he sounded distraught.

"Larry," he said on the recording, his voice breaking, "I really need a friend right now and you're the person who came to mind. Would you please call me back?"

So I called Bill and learned, between his sobs, that his fiancée had broken their engagement the night before. He was shattered. For the first time in his life, he had given himself wholeheartedly to a relationship with a woman, and then she'd disappointed him.

They had seemed perfect for each other. He was handsome and successful; she was a beautiful, well-known area model. Together, they looked like the plastic couple you see on the tops of wedding cakes. They were also both believers who shared the same faith.

Bill asked to meet with me. So, after work that evening I went over to his house and found him crying as hard as a man can cry. I've experienced the feeling of devastation which floods over a person when someone wonderful leaves his or her life. I understand what a shock it is.

Yet, I sensed God's presence in Bill's living room. And I knew I was the person who was supposed to be there for him. I stayed with Bill into the wee hours of the morning.

Like so many times in the past, God gave me a supernatural strength and energy to get by on less sleep than usual.

I told Bill, "I don't have a Band-Aid approach. I have too much respect for you to pat you on the shoulder and tell you everything is going to be OK. I know in my heart everything will be all right, but it's going to be a process, and it's going to be painful. One thing I can tell you from my own experience is that the secret of where I am in my life has everything to do with where God is in my life."

I explained what I went through after Tari left and how I got down on my knees to put God first. I also told Bill I would be glad to be his friend. I hadn't had a close male friend since Jack died so it seemed like God put us in each other's lives for a purpose.

Bill and I began to hang out with each other. For several weeks, all he could talk about was the ruined relationship and how his heart was broken. He needed to talk about those things. We prayed together regarding his situation, and I told him about what God was doing in my life through the downtown network of friends.

"I want to be involved with that," Bill said. "I want to show people there can be another godly man who can go out and have fun with the opposite sex, have integrity and the right agenda with them. I want to be part of what you're doing in Old Town."

Bill laughs when he says he hadn't been in a smoky bar or pool room for many years until he began to run around with me. But, as a result, he was introduced to the downtown group God has established in my life. I saw him begin to relax and smile again. I saw him open up to other people and I saw people reach out to him. He also became an important part of the Timberline Church singles ministry I led at the time in a volunteer capacity.

One day Bill called me. "I'd like to share my story with the singles group," he said, "tell them what God has done for me." Though I'd become better acquainted with Bill in recent weeks, I still didn't know a whole lot about him. So I was interested to hear what he had to say.

I knew he had been highly successful in the business world, pulling in a six-figure income for years. He wore the best suits, drove the best cars, owned the best houses, had the best of everything. By the world's standards, it looked like Bill had all it took to be successful. However, he told the singles a different story.

"This is difficult for me to talk about," he said, "but I want to tell you the process God has brought me through to get to this point in my spiritual life.

"From the time I was a little kid, my mom and dad made me go to church. It was a more formal church than this one is, and both my parents were actively involved in it. Ours was a very small town. Everybody in the church knew each other and everybody in the town knew each other.

"When I was a young man I got involved in a relationship with a woman that was displeasing to my parents and displeasing to those in the church. Looking back, I probably should not have gotten into the situation, but I was young. It was painful to break away from that friendship. When I did, instead of receiving the support of my loved ones and those in the church, I was ostracized because I hadn't lined up with their expectations.

"It made me bitter, angry, and withdrawn. I took a high paying job clear across the country in southern Florida to get away from my family, my church, and my town. I had a lucrative position and material success in

West Palm Beach, an exclusive, fast-paced area. Everybody at work thought I really had my stuff together.

"Little did they know that, because of the pain I had endured back home and because I had withdrawn from emotional contact with people, I had lost my ability to trust anyone. I had become a one-man island, working 60 to 80 hours a week, eating alone at fancy restaurants.

"I lived in Florida for two years without cultivating close friends. I didn't establish any relationships other than surface ones at work. On the outside it looked like I had everything together but on the inside I was really hurting. I was lonely and dying.

"I couldn't sleep at night. I would often walk in the condo parking lot until three, four, five o'clock in the morning, and then maybe fall into a fitful sleep for a couple hours. My insides churned. I didn't feel like I had a purpose for living. I was a classic workaholic who escaped through work, totally withdrawing from family and potential friendships.

"When I moved to Colorado a few years ago, I still had all the pain, and all those unresolved hurts. Larry has cut my hair for years but he hasn't heard this story. He's had no way of knowing the torment I was in. I was bitter toward anything affiliated with church or religion until I came back to God through Marilyn's invitation to Timberline.

"In time, I began to realize there is a God who cares about me and I can be healed of so many things. I have been in the process of healing, but, when my fiancée broke our engagement recently, it was the most agonizing of all the painful things I have gone through. I about went over the edge again.

"So God sent Larry into my life to be my best friend. We have talked, we have prayed together, we have gone out and walked his beat downtown. God is showing me He wants me to be like Larry in reaching out to people and showing who I am on the inside. I've experienced a lot of joy and peace from doing just that. And I have a contentment in my spirit I never had before, though I was considered successful in the business world."

Bill smiled. "That's what God has been doing in my life. Where He's placed me today, in my friendship with Larry and the people in this group and this church, I am now the happiest I've ever been. It's a God thing."

CHAPTER 12

THIS GOD THING

I met Jill the first time she came in for a haircut in the spring of 1994. She was 25 or 26 years old and studying to be a coach and a teacher. Jill is animated, talented, and charming—a very likable, blue-eyed blonde. She is also a strong-willed person who always says what's on her mind.

After I finished the cut, she said, "We should go out and do something sometime, have more time to talk." So we went to dinner a week or two later, swapped life stories and had a great time.

Because I want to be sensitive to people's needs and to the Holy Spirit, I prayed a silent prayer that night I often pray when I'm out with unbelievers: "God, is there something you want me to share with this person tonight? What is your schedule?" Even though I'm looking for an opportunity to talk with my friends about the Lord, a lot of times it doesn't happen right away. So it was to be with Jill.

We became good friends, spending many hours together shooting pool and going to movies. We also went out to dinner every two or three weeks and talked about some of the deeper aspects of life. Jill is very inquisitive, so the two of us discussed all kinds of interesting topics.

When we first met, Jill liked to party—a lot. She didn't want just a couple beers; she liked to really go for it. I also saw a neediness and addictiveness in her choices of boyfriends. The guys she dated usually didn't bring out the best in her.

We'd been hanging out together for two or three years, which shows the patience God often asks us to have with people, when the opportunity I had prayed and hoped for presented itself. At lunch one day Jill leaned toward me, her face serious.

"Larry," she said, "I just can't understand it. I have a nice apartment and a great car. I make good grades in school. I have lots of friends. We go out and have fun all the time. It seems like I have everything in the world going for me, like I'm right on track, but I feel empty inside, as if there's something missing."

Realizing this was a crucial moment for Jill, I reached across the table to put my hand on hers. "You know, Jill, we've had hundreds of hours of conversation over the last few years and I've wanted to talk about this for some time. You're right. You have everything outwardly that should make a person happy. Everything. You have the American dream and when you get your degree you'll continue the dream with an all-American career.

"Years ago, a great writer said there is a God-shaped space in the soul of every human that only the Lord can fill. I submit this to you, with all the respect in the world— I believe God is the only thing you're lacking in your life."

Jill just stared at me and rubbed her chin. Finally, she said, "I'm going to have to think about that one for awhile." So we finished our meal, I gave her a hug, and we went our separate ways.

The next Saturday afternoon the phone rang. It was Jill—strong, independent Jill—asking, "Larry, what's the name of that church you go to?"

I told her.

"Here's what I've decided to do," she said. "I'm going to that church tomorrow morning. Tell me what times the services are held."

I told her all the service times.

"Which one are you going to?" she asked.

I told her which one.

"I love you, Lar, and I like spending time with you, but I'm going to a different service. I want to do this on my own." She added, "I'm taking a notebook and I'm gonna find out what's happening over there with this God thing."

I laughed to myself because it was a typical Jill move. She had to do it her own way. She is not easily swayed by anybody, for which I admire her. The next morning came and went. I didn't see Jill. Of course, my curiosity was aroused.

So I decided to eat lunch and watch the ball game at the restaurant where she worked part-time. Shortly after I placed my order, Jill came around. We hugged each other and talked about the ball game. After we had small-talked for several minutes, she put her hands on her waist, glared at me and said, "You gonna ask me about church or not?"

"Yeah, but I wanted to wait until you were ready to talk about it," I chuckled.

"Well, I liked it. OK? That guy is a really good speaker and I'm going back again. I don't know what will become of all this but it has piqued my interest and I'll be going back."

Then she smiled. "Thank you, Larry. Thank you for inviting me. Thank you for letting me know there's a place like Timberline."

Jill has not had the dramatic transformation Nikki did. We're talking about a person who seemed to have it all together and wasn't in dire straits or so far away from God you could see it in her behavior. Yet, just like all of us, she desperately needed Him in her life.

She has grown spiritually, her drinking and partying days are past tense, and she just married a great guy. She also finished her studies at Colorado State University and is now teaching and coaching at a junior high school. She loves her new job.

My friend Jill writes the most original and unique cards and letters. At least once a month she drops me a thoughtful note. The following card describes the value of long term friendships:

Dear Larry—Here's to our lasting friendship...

Some people are fortunate enough to meet someone special in their lives who, even though he or she may follow a separate way, continues to share a lasting friendship. The special times spent together, the people and places shared, are memories they will both have. These are friends who are always remembered...those who live in the heart no matter what...always just a thought or phone call away.

Know that, even if years come between us, this card is given to you, my special friend, with love and care.

Thank you for being a vital part of my life, and for being the unique essence of a lasting friendship. I'm so grateful for your friendship. Please don't ever think I take you for granted.

Love, Jill

CHAPTER 13

I LIKE YOU

One night I was out with some new believers from my church. They wanted to go dancing after dinner, so we went to Linden's in Old Town to dance to live music. I know most of the people in the restaurants and bars downtown, but that night I saw a new waitperson at Linden's.

Since I like to meet people and make new friends, I introduced myself and learned the young woman's name was Janessa. I asked how long she'd been working at Linden's. She told me she'd been tending bar and waiting tables there for just a few weeks.

Janessa was bubbly and outgoing. She had blonde, waist-length hair, had been a Colorado University cheerleader and had worked in bars off and on from the time she turned 21 years old. She was a fun-loving, dynamic young lady. We joked and kidded with each other throughout the evening. And, as we were leaving, I said, "Hey, Janessa, it's really been nice to meet you. I hope to see you around again pretty soon."

"You probably won't," she responded. "I've been bartending and running drinks for the last eight or nine years off and on. I thought I could do it again, but I can't. The guys hit on you, the women hate you, people spill things on you, sometimes they're rude—and we're never tipped good enough. I'm getting too old for this, so I doubt I'll be here much longer."

We'd made a connection and I hated to lose touch with her; yet, I knew it was true she would be constantly hit on in that type of environment. So I said, "Well, look, I'm glad we met and I just want to tell you this. I cut hair right down the street. If you ever need a good haircut and/or a good friend, just come down and see Larry."

We looked each other in the eye, shook hands and she said, with a smile, "I just might do that."

I have a lot of those kinds of encounters, so I didn't think anything more about our evening at Linden's. But, one afternoon when I returned from a walk around downtown, there was Janessa sitting in my chair. "You had a cancellation," she announced. Then she added, "You told me a couple months ago if I ever needed a good haircut and a good friend, to come see Larry. So here I am."

We visited while I cut her hair and became better acquainted. When she paid for her cut, she took one of my cards and wrote her phone number on the back. "I don't usually give this out," she said, "but we should get together and do something sometime. I like you."

I felt this little inward smile I always get when someone says, "I like you." People don't know what draws them to me but I know it's God's Spirit and I knew I'd be calling her soon.

Actually, I called her the next day. "Hey, Janessa, how's that haircut working out?"

"The haircut is great!" she responded. "But you knew that. You want something else. You want to go out because we had so much fun yesterday."

I said, "Yeah, I do. But I'm sure someone like you is booked up several weeks in advance."

"We could go out tonight if you'd like. Want to go to dinner?"

"Sounds good."

We both got dressed up, went to dinner together and swapped life stories—the usual. From previous experiences, I could tell my connection with Janessa was spiritual. Later that evening we shot pool, laughed a lot and had fun.

The next day we were in touch again. Janessa said, "I sure enjoy hanging out with you. You want to go out again this weekend?"

"I'd love to."

When we met again, in the midst of our conversation Janessa suddenly said, "You know what? I want to marry a guy just like you."

I grinned, feeling 10 feet tall.

But then she added, "Of course, quite a bit younger." We laughed and laughed. Still, it was a nice compliment and I was honored she felt I had the qualities she was looking for in a husband. And, again, I knew it was God within me attracting her.

Later, she asked me a question which still makes me laugh. "What would you think about dating somebody a lot younger than yourself?"

"Well," I responded, "there would be some serious things to consider, such as me leaving the table in a restaurant to use the bathroom and the waiter asking, 'Would you like to wait until your father gets back to order?'"

We had a good chuckle over that mental picture. God has blessed me with youthful energy and appearance, but I just knew something similar would happen if I dated a woman that much different in age. I added, "Another problem I can foresee is going home to meet the parents and discovering they're the same age I am." We laughed some more.

I asked Janessa about her dreams and goals. "I want the classic house with the picket fence and the kids running around the yard." She smiled. "And, of course, a successful husband, one who treats me like a queen."

As we talked, I realized, though I would love to be with somebody like Janessa and though she wanted to be with a younger version of a guy like me, there would be no romance in our friendship. And I knew Janessa sensed that as well.

We spent a lot of time together the next couple of months. I was always looking for an opportunity to offer her Jesus but when I mentioned my faith to her, she didn't reach out and grab it or ask to know more. However, I knew she loved music and I knew the church Christmas musical was coming up. Timberline Church has tremendous programs which reach into the community, events you can bring your friends to. So I said, "Hey, Janessa, you like good Christmas music?"

"I love it!" she exclaimed. "I used to sing in a school choir and I'm a hopeless romantic when it comes to Christmas."

"Great!" I said. "We've got this really neat Christmas musical going on over at the church. How about we go there on Saturday night and then to dinner afterwards?"

"That sounds wonderful."

Saturday evening, we dressed up and went to church. As always, God's Spirit was there and the presentation was powerful. Afterwards, Dary shared a story about why Jesus had to come down from heaven into our environment and walk among us as He did.

The story goes something like this: A grandfather went to visit his daughter and his two-year-old grandson. When he arrived, he found his grandchild sobbing in the playpen, confined for disobedience. As soon as his grandpa walked in, the little boy reached up to him, crying, "Out, Gwampa, out!"

It was hard for the grandfather because he was torn. He loved his daughter and wanted to respect her discipline. He knew she had put her son in the playpen for a good reason. Yet, his heart was broken because he longed to reach down, pick up the child, squeeze him tight, and make everything better.

The man was in a terrible quandary, wanting to do the right thing. Finally, a brilliant idea occurred to him. He crawled into the playpen with the toddler, sat down, pulled him close, dried his tears and smothered him with kisses.

And that's what Jesus did for us. Our holy God has a perfect standard for humanity to live by in order to have communion and closeness with Him. But it's impossible for sinful men to live up to God's standard, no matter how hard we try.

So God the Father, in His great love, came up with the ultimate solution to the dilemma, which was "crawling into the playpen" by sending His Son Jesus to live with us and die for us. Jesus' death provided forgiveness for sin and, therefore, holiness to those willing to repent of their sins and accept his cleansing and forgiveness. As a result, we can have an amazing, intimate relationship with a holy, loving God.

Janessa took in every word of the story. When the pastor asked if anybody wanted to accept the Lord, out of the corner of my eye I saw her hand go up. And I saw her tears. I knew God had touched her.

Afterwards, we had a great time at dinner, then decided to go to a movie. There was a film showing at the time called *The Preacher's Wife*. The story is about an angel who is sent from heaven in the form of a well-dressed, good-looking, young man in a tan suit. His assignment is to help a struggling young pastor and his wife and family. They are trying to fulfill their responsibilities in life but have drifted apart and are missing out on the joys of their family relationships.

After becoming their friend and doing all the angelic things he is supposed to do—spending time with the pastor, the wife, the kids—the angel is attracted to the wife. There is a scene toward the end of the movie where he is alone in the family's living room, looking at a wedding picture of the preacher and his wife. In a moment of weakness, the angel envisions himself in the picture instead of the husband. Instantly, thunder from heaven jolts him from his daydream. The angel is, of course, humbled and repentant.

At that point in the movie Janessa touched my arm. "That's you, isn't it?" she whispered.

"I never thought of it before," I whispered back, "but you're right. God wants me to keep my focus on what my relationships are all about."

Janessa has been a joy in my life. She has grown in the Lord and was the one who typed my teaching notes for me when I led the singles group.

Upon graduation from Colorado State University with a degree in animal science, she was hired at the Cheyenne Mountain Zoo in Colorado Springs, Colorado. She's always wanted to work in a zoo and is very happy in her new position.

CHAPTER 14

THE JOY OF MY LIFE

Don's story (name changed) goes back about 25 years. He was a customer of mine at a barbershop I worked at in Ohio. Haircuts in the old-fashioned barbershop only took about 10 minutes compared with styling hair today which takes 30 to 40 minutes.

Yet, Don and I became friends. We ate lunch together now and then, went out occasionally in the evening; we even went fishing together once. As we talked about our lives, I let him know I was a believer and told him I had a strong faith.

Don's response was, "What do you mean by that?" Don was a nice guy but he wanted to analyze my faith and argue about it. He was successful, articulate and educated, with a respect for intellect and philosophy, but not for the Gospel. Christianity was too simplistic for him.

"I thought you were a lot more intelligent than that, Larry," he said. "You are well read, a good conversationalist, and open-minded. How can you possibly believe that stuff?"

I was raised in an argumentative family but have always felt it wrong to argue about religion and the Bible, so

I didn't react to Don's barbs. We can have discussions, but we have to be careful. Some of the greatest conflicts in history occurred because people took sides in the name of religion or Christianity. I don't want to be a part of that.

Don and I had some pretty heavy talks for a couple of years. Our conversations were often about Christianity. He was obviously intrigued yet he adamantly refused to accept the Gospel, reminding me of the old saying, "Methinks he doth protest too much." Don was so intent on trying to disprove my faith, I knew God was working in his heart.

One day he said, "I want to be open-minded. I want to see what you're talking about. I'm going to your church with you." Don insisted on sitting at the front so he could hear the preacher, hear the singing and see what was happening. So that's where we sat, Don with his arms crossed the entire service.

At that particular time, I was attending a charismatic church where the Holy Spirit was manifested openly and abundantly. People would pray around the altars; there was shouting, raising of hands, individuals receiving various gifts of the Holy Spirit and displaying them. The altar call at the end of this particular service was long, loud and rambunctious.

I'm sure it was an extreme, shocking experience for Don, but he was mesmerized by the power displayed. As we left the church, he said, "Something was going on in there. I don't know what it was but it didn't seem like anything that can be explained psychologically."

The church service obviously impressed Don; yet, interestingly enough, we didn't discuss Christianity again for a long time. We still went to lunch or shot pool but he evidently didn't feel like talking about God. Poor Don probably got a bigger dose of church than he was looking for.

Then he was transferred to California. And we lost touch with each other when I moved to Colorado. So it was quite a surprise to get a call from Don one evening several years later. "Larry!" he exclaimed. "This is Don from Ohio. Do you remember me?"

"I sure do."

"I've had the most difficult time tracking you down!" he said. "Been working for weeks trying to get your phone number." Then he said, "I have the best news for you! My wife and I accepted the Lord and so did our children. My faith is now the joy of my life! I cannot begin to tell you what it means to me.

"If you had not had the courage, the fortitude, and the persistence to hang in there when I kept trying to argue with you, I probably wouldn't have come this far." He paused. "Remember the time you took me to church?"

I laughed. "I'll never forget it!"

Don chuckled too. "I was so analytical and so against wanting to believe, but you planted the seed and others watered it. Now, my whole family goes to church every weekend. I had to share that with you. It's the greatest thing that's ever happened to me."

CHAPTER 15

I LOVE YOU

One of the friends I have the most fun with is a young lady I met at the Rio in August of 1995. I had gone there to see a friend of mine I call California Carl (name changed), a really neat guy who had moved to Colorado from California a few months earlier.

Carl is about my age and I like him a lot; he's a great guy. I could never walk into the Rio without him giving me a handshake or a hug. He had recently gone through a divorce, so we had that in common and had become friends. I'd even been able to talk with him about the Lord a time or two.

That night Carl said, "Come on over here Larry and meet a friend I just met at the festival we had downtown last week. Her name is Sherri." So I met Sherri, a young woman with long, light brown hair. She was outspoken and a little on the loud side. She also seemed rather opinionated. I thought, *Oh boy, here's a little fireball.*

Carl said, "Hey, Larry is a hair cutter. Maybe you can have him cut your hair sometime."

"Get away from me!" she declared. "I don't want a haircut. I've been letting this grow out for years."

But, women do like to talk about their hair when they get around people like me. Curiosity gets the best of them. After we'd visited with Carl for 15 or 20 minutes, Sherri suddenly turned to me and said, "Just in theory now, what would you do with my hair?"

"Well," I said, "instead of having it all one length, I would put some long layers in it and frame it around your face. Cutting it around your face would show off your features, bring out your eyes and cheekbones. But I would leave the length in the back."

"Really?" she said. "You'd do all that but you wouldn't take any off the length?"

"That's right."

"When do you have an opening?" she asked.

"I'm booked for the next four or five days but I'm sure we can work something out."

"Now you've got me really wanting to do it."

"Oh, come on," I said. "Let's just go do it now." So I took her across the street right then—must have been 10:00 P.M.—and cut her hair. Afterwards we went back to the Rio with her new look. Several people at the bar had been watching the whole thing, so they applauded the after look.

Sherri and I were having such a good time we decided to go to Old Chicago for a bite to eat. As we visited, my impression was that Sherri was attractive but down on life, down on relationships. She drank too much and appeared to be an unhappy person with a lot of pain in her life. Even though we talked for several hours, I didn't expect to spend a lot of time with her in the future.

However, a couple days later she stopped by the salon and asked, "Hey, you want to go over to the Rio?" And that's how our friendship began. Every once in awhile we would shoot pool or go out dancing, but I still did not feel the spiritual connection I feel with a lot of people when I first meet them. As positive as I was at that stage of my life, she was negative, which didn't give us much common ground.

I learned Sherri and her mother had been abandoned by her father and taken in by her grandparents when she was very young. Although Sherri's mother eventually married a man who provided a stable home for both herself and her daughter, Sherri still suffered the scars of abandonment. She was afraid of intimacy in relationships, of verbally communicating her feelings and being open to others. And she drank herself into oblivion almost every night trying to escape the hurt.

But God began to work in Sherri's life. Over time, I saw another person develop. I saw a softer side, a less negative side, a more fun side.

Through friendship and encouragement, Sherri has blossomed and progressed from being a confused young lady to becoming a self-confident woman. She has learned how to open up and be charming and how to use her incredible smile to make others feel special. Below is a card Sherri sent me not long ago which explains a little about how God worked in our relationship:

> Everyone should have a friend like you. You're so much fun to be with and you're such a good person. You can crack me up with laughter and touch my heart with your kindness. You have that wonderful ability to know when to offer advice and when to just sit still in quiet support.
>
> Time after time you've come to my rescue and brightened so many of my routine days. And time after time I've realized how fortunate I am that my life includes you. I really do believe everyone should have a friend like you. But, so far, it looks like you're one of a kind.
>
> Love, Sherri

I had a strong desire to share the Gospel with Sherri. She had not been raised in church; and, because of circumstances in her childhood, she had been disappointed by what she saw of the church. She'd also had negative encounters with hypocritical and judgmental Christians.

I try to be cautious when I share my faith but I knew I had to be doubly so with Sherri. She was sure she didn't need church, Christians, or God in her life. So I prayed, "God, open the door so I can share with Sherri. She's such a special friend."

Then I learned Timberline's Easter passion play attendance had grown to the point where the church needed to rent the Lincoln Center, a community auditorium. Sherri, who had maintained she would go anywhere with me except to church, agreed to go to the Lincoln Center to watch the passion play.

Afterwards I said, "Thanks for going with me." Sherri didn't say a word; she showed no emotion whatsoever. However, after church on Easter Sunday, I dropped by her parents' house and heard her in the other room talking about the play, saying how much she enjoyed it.

I was the one who introduced Sherri to Rick who recently became her husband. I've known Rick for years. He is a neat guy and a four-time world hacky-sack champion. He's also a busy car salesman who works evenings. Before their marriage, Sherri and I often ate dinner together while he was at work.

Rick used to say, "I'm glad Sherri has someone to spend time with. I feel guilty working late and leaving her alone." Since their marriage, however, they are finding ways to spend more time together.

In the months before the wedding, I was able to bring up the subject of faith more and more with Sherri, to talk about spiritual things. One day she said, "I think I like the Jesus you talk about."

Then, shortly after that, the neatest thing happened. A couple of friends from Boulder, Melissa and Anna, came in for haircuts. Sherri was also in the salon that afternoon getting her hair colored. When everyone was finished, Melissa said, "Hey, let's all go over to the Rio." So the four of us walked across the street to the restaurant.

As we visited, Sherri and I joked and kidded around, giving each other a hard time. The other two said, "You guys have the most incredible friendship." They could see we were great friends even though Sherri was obviously happily engaged.

Sherri grinned. "I hate to say this in front of Larry, but ever since I met him good things have been happening in my life."

Just like on cue, the two young women got up, leaned over on each side of Sherri and hugged her cheek to cheek. "Honey," one of them said, "don't you realize Larry has brought God into your life?"

Sherri looked at me and smiled. "I believe you're right; it's true. Larry did bring God into my life." My heart skipped a beat. I had prayed for that moment for almost three years.

Sherri is doing great in her personal life and in her marriage. The following is a letter I wrote to her to express my feelings for her as well as to give her a tool to explain our unique friendship to anyone who might ask:

Dear Sherri,

I love you. I have for a long time. I know you're not surprised because I tell you that every time we see each other. There are many kinds of love, and each of us has a tremendous capacity to love a lot of different people in our lifetimes.

Unfortunately, the most popular concept of love in our present culture is limited to just a few preconceived ideas such as love between family members, romantic love (specifically the physical kind), and love for our pets or material possessions. These standard perceptions are reinforced by movies, television, music and the shallow, superficial view society has of love today.

The modern concept of romantic love it seems is "I want you," "I need you," "I can't live without you." The main emphasis being on the word "I" indicating a selfish need to be with someone because they make us feel good (turn us on, do things for us, etc.). I admit this is the most popular definition of love now, but it is not the highest form.

I believe the highest love to be a much more unselfish one that basically says I love you even when you don't do things for me all the time. It says I love you because you are you. And I want to be a part of your life to help make it the best it can possibly be. That special kind of love is expressed by us doing something for those we love just because of the smile we can bring to his or her face.

Sherri, that is the way I love you. It's a God-given love I can't even completely understand myself. You have been a tremendous friend and companion the past couple of years. We have shared so many special times. You've made my sides ache from laughing at your unique sense of humor and, no matter how long I live, I'll never forget your incredible smile that lights up a room anywhere we go. We've shared our histories with each other, our hopes, dreams, disappointments, heartaches, and so much else.

You and Rick are in a committed relationship and nobody respects those boundaries more than I do. I really love and care about Rick, too. I've seen him grow in so many ways the past few years. He's a great guy. If you two nurture an unselfish, unconditional love for each other, you'll be together for a long, long time. I pray that both of you will have happy and fulfilling lives.

I thank God every day for the wonderful people in my life. You are a dear and precious friend. We both have busy lives, but let's always make the time to stay in touch. If you could only know how happy you make me feel when you surprise me by stopping by or call to say hello. I want you to know those little things put a smile on my face and make my life a lot better by your being a part of it. Thanks for everything you do.

I Love You!!
Lar, Your Best Friend

CHAPTER 16

THE LAR WHO CARES

I've played pool with Joe (name changed) for years. He's one of the top players in town and a good friend. Just recently I learned he and a mutual friend of ours call me "The Lar Who Cares." They think my lifestyle is humorous—all the people I hang out with, all the friends I have. It's been a joke with them, "Hey, I wonder who 'The Lar Who Cares' is going out with tonight?"

One night, however, it was Joe I was out with and Joe who needed care. He had been struggling through some hard times and wanted to talk. Since his teen years, Joe has had a history of drug and alcohol abuse. He's been in and out of several expensive rehabilitation programs, intensive ones, without much success.

That night Joe told me about the nickname but said they knew it was a God thing. Plus, he acknowledged, maybe it was time for him to try God for himself. "I'm here because I feel like you're a real person," he said. "You're someone I can relate to; you've been around the block.

"I've watched you for a long time, Larry," he added. "You've survived a lot of adversity and tragedy and somehow managed to land on your feet every time and stay out of addictions. What's your secret?"

I responded, "Since you're asking, Joe, I'm telling. You know my secret—it's my faith; it's God." Then I shared stories with him about how putting God at the center of my existence changed my life and the lives of other friends who put Him first. As I talked, I saw tears in his eyes and knew God was working in his heart.

Joe told me he had attended Timberline Church the night before with a friend who was also addictive, someone I didn't know. "Larry," he said, "I felt something there I've never felt before."

"Do you want that kind of power in your life on a regular basis, Joe?" I asked him.

"I do."

So we went to the salon, which was fast becoming a downtown temple, knelt down and prayed. Joe turned his life over to God then and there. Not long after that decision, he was married and now has a little one on the way. Joe is getting a handle on his addictions and doing better than ever before in his life.

CHAPTER 17

TAKING THE CHALLENGE

One Sunday afternoon shortly after Nikki became a believer, I stopped by a tuxedo rental place in the mall. I needed to get measurements for my daughter Kim's upcoming wedding in Ohio. The store was crowded. Must have been a dozen people in that small shop.

One of the employees, a young woman, came over to me. She had blue eyes, short blonde hair and looked like she'd just stepped out of *Vogue* magazine. "May I help you, sir?" she asked.

"I feel guilty asking," I said. "I just need to be measured for a tux for my daughter's wedding in another state. Maybe I should return later when you guys aren't quite so busy."

She said, "You come with me. I'll take care of you right now." We visited as she worked and I soon had a feeling she was going to be one of those special people in my life.

After she finished taking my measurements, I looked at her name tag and said, "Amanda, I cut hair for a living and whoever cuts your hair is doing a good job. So, I don't mean to be presumptuous, but to thank you for helping me out and taking time to do this for me, I'd like to give you a free haircut."

Amanda is smart, precise and sarcastic, with a cutting sense of humor. She responded, "Are you any good?"

Not wanting to sound arrogant but knowing I needed to convince her, I answered as modestly as I could, "I'm pretty good."

She said, "OK, I'll take your word for it."

I wrote down the salon information for her. Within a couple weeks she came in for a haircut. When we did the consultation, I discovered that the man who had cut her hair when she was growing up in Chicago was the man who had done the majority of my training 24 years earlier.

His name is Mario, and he's one of the top hair stylists in the world. He and his staff do makeovers for numerous movie stars and other celebrities. So Amanda and I made a connection through Mario right away.

As I cut her hair and we joked around, I said, "We might have to go to out lunch or over to the Rio sometime; just go out and have some fun."

Amanda's response was, "Like I'd really go out with an old timer like you!" But she laughed as she said it.

"Yeah, well, whatever. Call me in a couple days and let me know how you like the haircut."

"Oh, don't worry. I'll be sure to let you know!" She did call me in a couple days to tell me she liked the cut. Sometime later that week, I stopped in to see her at the mall.

"What are you doing Friday night?" she asked.

"My plans are flexible."

"Let's go out and get some dinner."

I laughed. "You're going to forget the old man thing now, huh."

"Nah," she said. "I'm not going to forget it but we'll go out anyway."

After that night, we got together every couple of weeks and developed a lot of mutual friends. I looked for opportunities to share the Lord with Amanda though she was a young lady from an affluent background who seemed uninterested in spiritual things. Many times people like her don't realize they have a spiritual need.

Yet I knew that everyone, no matter the background, needs God. Over time I was able to explain how my network of friends had been developed through God working in and through my life and that I attended a really fun church. Her response was always, "That's nice. I'm glad for you."

About a month before Jami's accident in 1995, I introduced Jami and Amanda. They liked each other instantly. Later, when Amanda learned Jami had passed away, she said, "Larry, you will come over to my house for dinner every night this week. I'll cook for you; we'll get your favorite movies. I'll put my arms around you and be your friend. This is the time you need to let somebody help you."

What a special week that was. The day before the funeral we went to the mall to buy a tie. Amanda insisted on helping. "I need to pick out your tie for the funeral because you might mess it up if you choose it yourself!"

She drove me to the funeral service and we sat together on the front row. That evening, we went to an informal memorial for Jami at a friend's house. As we left, Amanda said, "You know, it's Friday night and we're all dressed up. If Jami were here with us now we'd probably all go down to Old Chicago to see some of our friends."

"Yeah, you're right. That's what we'd do."

Amanda smiled. "Let's go down there anyway, Larry. As hard as it is to be around other people, let's just go down there for a little bit. I think it would be a good thing for us to end the night on that note."

Our time at Old Chicago was emotional, but God had good things planned. As we talked, a nice-looking young guy came up and visited with us. He introduced himself, said his name was Brian. After a few minutes Amanda excused herself.

As she walked away, Brian asked, "Are you guys seeing each other or anything like that?"

"Absolutely not," I replied. "I've got kids older than she is. We're just friends who care a lot about each other."

"I'm interested in her. I'd sure like to take her out."

"Well, I'll tell you something, Brian," I said. "She is one of the finest, neatest, people I've ever met but, unless you have a backbone like a saw log, she will chew you up and spit you out. She is one strong-willed woman."

"I like that," he responded. "I'll take the challenge."

When Amanda came back, I made myself scarce and they got into a heavy conversation. Brian asked her out. A week or two later, they went skiing together and a couple years later, they were married in Chicago.

Amanda and Brian's wedding at the Medinah Country Club, one of the more prestigious places in the country, was the most glamorous I'd ever seen. The ballroom is so huge and beautiful it takes your breath away. And the wedding was the only one I've been to where everybody, including the guests, wore tuxes or evening gowns.

At the reception, the bride and groom danced the first dance together and the parents danced the second dance with Amanda and Brian. Then, the band began to play Jami's favorite song, "The Dance" by Garth Brooks. Amanda's eyes searched the crowd and, in that large room filled with friends and relatives, picked me out, crooked her finger and mouthed, "You come here."

We danced cheek to cheek, tears in our eyes, Amanda whispering, "This one is for Jami and this one is for you." I was reminded again what a huge heart that classy young woman has. It was her big moment, her special day, and she was thinking of me.

Amanda and Brian were married several years ago. Like I pray for others in my network of friends who haven't become believers yet, I've prayed for those two. "God," I have pleaded, "I love these people; they are family to me. When are they going to become believers? I want them to go to heaven with me. I want them to be part of my spiritual family."

Not long ago I drove to Denver to see Brian and Amanda and their new baby boy. Earlier, I had given Amanda the rough draft of the first three or four chapters of this book to read. As we visited, we talked about the book.

"Those chapters made a big impact on me, Larry," said Amanda. "Your story helped bring me to a point I've been thinking about for a long time. When the time is right, I want to talk some more about those things you are writing about."

A couple weeks later Brian and Amanda called. "Can we come up and spend time with you this weekend?" they asked. I was delighted to have them visit.

On Saturday night we went to the Rio and Old Chicago, of course—even took the baby. We had a terrific time. In the midst of the fun I thought, *wouldn't it be great if I could have Amanda and Brian sit beside me in church sometime.*

As the evening wrapped up, Amanda said, "Before we go back to our motel, let's make plans for tomorrow because we'd like to spend the whole day with you."

"Well," I said, "I'm going to the 9:45 service at my church."

Amanda said, "So are we."

Sitting next to Brian and Amanda and their baby boy, I thanked God for His faithfulness and His hand on their lives. After the service, they said, "That was great! This is what we want in our lives. Will you come down and help us find a good church in Denver?"

I nodded and smiled, thinking, *God is good—so good.*

CHAPTER 18

THE SECRET OF LIFE

We have a fairly new restaurant in Old Town called Austin's. I've known the owners—who operate another restaurant in Fort Collins—for years. When they started Austin's, they hired a young blonde guy with piercing blue eyes to run the bar. His name was James and he became the heart and soul of the restaurant. He was a friendly, out-going, charismatic person in his mid-twenties who went out of his way to recognize people and make them feel special.

On opening day, the owners invited me in and unofficially declared me "Austin's Number One Customer." James was right in the middle of that bantering and he and I hit it off. Anytime I went into the restaurant or sat outside on the patio, James made a special point to speak to me, or at least put his hand on my shoulder.

James was curious about all my friends. "I've been watching you, Larry," he said one day. "You're a fascinating fellow. You've got a lot of friends and you have a really interesting life.

"Plus," he added, "you are always in a good mood; seems like you're constantly surrounded by people and having fun.

You've got something different going on and I'm gonna find out about it."

He was busy with his job at that moment, so it was not a good time to share the Gospel with him. However, when people weren't around, I said, "James, my unique life has everything to do with my faith in God." And I told him about my paralysis and the other tragedies I'd been through.

"At the core of all that," I said to him, "I learned to survive and to prosper through adversity. It all has to do with my faith. And the love God has put in my life is the reason I have all these friends. The love I have is a God thing."

"Larry," James responded, "I'd like to get with you some night and really talk about some of this stuff."

"I'd love that, James. Any time you want to talk you let me know. We'll do it." I saw something in him I've seen in a lot of people. I could tell that, even though he was outgoing and friendly, James was searching for God. I could see it in his eyes, in the questions he asked me, in the way he reached out to me.

James was an artist. He also read all kinds of books on philosophy, had quite a collection of music and was continually taking in information. He reminded me of the Scripture that says, "ever learning, and never able to come to the knowledge of the truth." I couldn't wait to talk with him about the things I knew he longed for in life; and I felt like that time was quickly approaching.

Shortly after our conversation, I went to the 5:30 church service on a Saturday night. When I left at 7:00 I was fired up and ready for action, so I decided to go downtown. As I stood in front of the salon about 7:30, two young ladies from the Austin's wait staff came running up to me. They threw their arms around me, crying, "Do you know what happened?"

"No," I said, puzzled by their behavior. "What happened? What's wrong?"

Through sobs they told me, "James killed himself last night."

I was shocked. Even though James and I had not spent a lot of time together, we had made a strong connection. My first thought was, *Wow, it's only been a couple of weeks since he said, "Let's get together sometime real soon, Larry. I want to talk to you about life."*

But I knew better than to fall into the guilt trap of thinking, *Why didn't I push it, why didn't I get with James before it was too late?* I wished with all my heart I'd had an opportunity to share the Gospel with him. Yet, what James had done was done and all I could do was be ready to be used by God to help others in the aftermath of his death.

The two young women invited me to go next door where the staff was gathering. Austin's owners had closed the restaurant and there were 30 to 40 staff members in the bar next to the salon, all young people in their 20s. They were in shock, crying and moaning, hugging each other and asking, "Why? What's this all about? Why James?"

To my amazement, when I walked in many of them ran up to me like I was their big brother. I hugged each of them and listened to what they had to say. I could tell God was working in the situation.

I had only met James' girlfriend once but we held each other close for a couple minutes. As she wiped her eyes, she said, "Larry, every day when James came home from work he talked about you. Not a day went by when he didn't mention you. He would say, 'Larry stopped by today,' or 'Larry walked by today.'

"Then he always added the same phrase. 'That guy has the answer to life; he knows the secret of life.' You were his hero, Larry. You were the person he looked up to."

I was overwhelmed. I knew James and I had connected and that we liked each other but I had no idea my life had affected him in such a way.

She added, "I would like to talk with you in the next few days."

"Sure," I said. "Anytime you want."

I was privileged to share with those young people and comfort them that night. And they comforted me. When they asked me to attend an upcoming private memorial service for James, I felt honored.

The day of the memorial service, I was in a prayerful attitude all day anticipating the 10:00 P.M. gathering. There were at least 50 people there, most of them young people who had worked with James in one restaurant or another. It wasn't a religious service; it was a memorial, an open forum with no agenda and James' favorite tunes playing in the background.

His girlfriend got up, shared a few thoughts about James, then said, "I want to open this up to anybody who would like to say what's on their mind and on their heart. We're going to stay around for as long as you have something to say."

One by one, several of James' closest friends got up and talked about him. I watched how different people handled his death. Those who didn't have a spiritual light on in their lives were obvious from the ways they were trying to cope and their lack of understanding of eternal things and how death related. Some tried to make the pain lighter through jokes and stories. Some broke down completely, weeping uncontrollably.

Finally, there was a lull and I knew it was my turn to speak to the group. *God help me to show You through my life tonight*, I prayed as I walked to the front of the room. When

I stood before them, I was aware of God's presence. He was with me and He was going to help me give them His comfort and peace.

As much as I wanted to shout out the secret James was searching for, I knew I couldn't say it all that night. Instead, I said, "James and I had a special friendship. He was the one who called me 'Austin's Number One Customer.'" The group nodded in agreement.

I said, "He told his girlfriend, 'Larry has the secret to life.' He told some of you that, too." More nods. "I won't go into detail now, but I believe I do know what the secret of life is and, if any of you ever want to talk with me about it, I'd be glad to share it with you.

"If James could be with us, he would want you to be reminded of a few things. You are sitting and standing there with your arms around each other, displaying a tremendous amount of love you never openly displayed before as strongly as you are right now. This is a special time in your lives. It's a hard time, but I want to tell you the love you're reaching out to each other with right now is part of that secret James talked about.

"And, if he were here I think he would want to say this, or at least want me to say it. As you go through life, love people with a love like this every day. Reach out to people and pretend each encounter might be the last time you ever see them. That will affect how you treat them.

"If you live your life that way, you won't come up short in your relationships. And, if you live every day of your life like it's your own last day, you will use your time on this earth to the fullest. If you keep those two thoughts in your mind throughout your life, then you will have keyed into some of the great secrets of life. I ask you to take James' spirit of friendship and love with you the rest of your lives.

"Thank you for letting me be a part of this memorial. I feel very honored to be here. I want you to know I will be available for each of you in the coming days and weeks. God bless you all."

That night, at least four or five of the young people came up to me. Two of them said, "We didn't believe in God before this happened but some people who are believers have been talking with us. They've told us what you're about. We want to spend time with you. We believe in God now and we want to take it further."

Not long after, a woman in our singles group at church donated some Bibles to the downtown outreach, saying, "Give these to whoever you think needs one." So I had the privilege of providing a Bible to each of those who expressed a desire to "take it further."

Through the tragedy of James' death, good things are happening at Austin's. In fact, one of the young ladies now regularly goes to church with me. God is working in hearts at that restaurant and I feel blessed to be a part of what He's doing there.

CHAPTER 19

BABY STEPS

I was at the Rio one night when I noticed two young women having a good time. So I walked over to their table and said, "You two have the most incredible smiles and you're having so much fun, I just had to come over and introduce myself."

I do that everywhere I go. It makes an impression on people. They think, *Here's someone who actually wants to know my name, who actually wants to know me.* I introduce myself probably 50 times a week and ask people their names.

The women said they were Sally and Yvonne (names changed). They also told me where they worked. So I called a couple days later to say, "Hi, you don't know it but I'm your new best friend." Sally, who had just gone through a divorce and was making new friends, suggested we get together for lunch.

At lunch, I could tell she was open to talking about spiritual things, so I told her about my *other job* downtown. She was very interested. "After I get back to work," she said, "I'm going to tell Yvonne about you because she's having some real struggles right now. Maybe you can help her."

One evening three or four weeks later, I was at Linden's but was strongly impressed around 9:30 to go to the Rio. I said to the friends I was with, "I have to go to the Rio right now, but I'll probably be back."

I strolled into the Rio and there at the end of the bar sat Sally and Yvonne. Their faces lit up when they saw me and they asked me to join them. As we gave each other a group hug, Yvonne burst into tears and clung to me like she was taking her last breath. It was a desperation hug, an I-really-need-to-talk-to-somebody hug, even though we didn't even know each other.

She said, "Sally says you're a strong Christian and she told me all about what you're doing when you're out here with people. She said your pastor calls you the 'Nightclub Evangelist'. I need someone like you to talk to. I'm really messed up. I've pushed God right out of my life.

"I've . . . I've been in . . . an affair for the last year," Yvonne continued, crying even harder. "I cooled off with God and let things creep in and then I ran into this guy who swept me off my feet. I left my husband who is a good man and who loves me. He is very upset with me for leaving him. Yet, I'm caught up in this affair and I don't want out of it . . . and God is so far out of my life."

Yvonne sat down, reached for her purse and pulled out a tissue. "I really do love God and I miss my relationship with Him. But my Christian friends are all saying, 'You gotta get your act together, go back to your husband and go back to church before you can go back to God.' They are so harsh and so judgmental I don't want to have anything to do with any of them."

I put my arm around Yvonne. "You know what," I said, "I've got some good news for you. God loves you just as much as He did when you were going to church every

Sunday. The Bible is very plain about that. He loves the drug addict as much as he loves the pastor of your church. That's what we humans can't understand. God is not keeping score. The Bible says there is not one righteous person, not one. God loves us just the way we are.

"God is not asking you to change your life. Just like you have this longing and yearning in your heart for God and you miss your relationship with Him, He is saying to you, 'I miss you. Will you please let me back in your life?' He's not asking you to throw everything away, but just to take Him back in your life.

"I'm not asking you," I continued, "and God is not asking you to change your whole life tonight, but to begin to take baby steps to come back to God."

"Can we get out of here?" Yvonne asked. The three of us walked out to her car.

Yvonne was crying as hard as I've seen anybody cry. She went through all the tissue in her purse. Finally I asked, "You want to go over to the salon where we can get some more tissue and some water?"

At the salon, she said, "Larry, I don't even know you but I can tell you anything. I didn't know they made Christians like you who can talk in a modern day language and be loving and caring and nonjudgmental."

"That's who God is making me into," I told her. "That's what He's been working on in my life for a long time."

It was obvious Yvonne was really addicted to her boyfriend emotionally and physically and yet God gave me a love for her. I didn't think, *Here's a backslidden Christian who is out of her marriage and in an affair, so I don't want to have anything to do with her.* Unfortunately, that's the way many Christians would react.

The Lord told me that night to just love her and let her know through my love how much He loves her. After two hours of talking, a box of tissue and a couple quarts of water, she said, "I feel so much better, like I've got this big load lifted off of me. I feel like I can have a relationship with God again."

"You better believe you can!" I said. "Do you want to pray together?"

"Would you please?"

We got down on our knees and I prayed against the enemy who was telling her she couldn't have a relationship with God. I also prayed she would take the baby step of letting God back into her life by asking, 'God will you please lead me and direct me and help me. Show me the way and give me the courage to do it.'"

The next day, Yvonne left a message thanking me for our time together but I didn't hear anything more from her. Finally, after a couple weeks, I called and left a message on her voice mail at work. "Yvonne, you've got so many things going on in your life with your husband, your job, your boyfriend, with your other life. I know you don't have time for us to be together, but I want you to know I'm praying for you every day.

"The night we talked was a turning point in your life. I know you and God are going to get back to where you once were because you have a heart for Him and that's what you want. If you ever need to call me, even if it's three in the morning, I'll be there for you.

"We don't have to see each other although that was a special, special evening we had together. God put us in each other's lives for that moment and I'm still here for you day or night. I just want you to know God is there all the time, and I am, too."

Three weeks later I was out walking my beat in the middle of the day and got this strong impression to call Yvonne at work. When I got back to the shop, I called her and said, "This is your new best friend and you don't even know it."

"Larry, is that you?" she exclaimed. "I'm so glad you called! I have to tell you something. There are people all around my desk, but I don't care who hears it. God is now in my life 100 percent. I broke off the affair and I'm back with my husband. I will never turn away from God again.

"My husband and I obviously have to work through some things and I know it won't be easy. But, he's a wonderful man and I believe we can do it with God's help. Thank you, Larry!"

CHAPTER 20

AND THE BEAT GOES ON

One Saturday night I went to the 5:30 church service and afterward decided to walk my beat. So I headed downtown, strolled through the Rio, talked with a few people in the network, just caught up with some folks; probably stuck around there for about an hour. Then I went over to Old Chicago and visited with three or four people there.

As I left Old Chicago, I decided to head for Linden's a couple blocks away which meant that as soon as I exited the building I needed to turn left. When I stepped out the door, however, I felt this compulsion to turn to the right instead.

So I took a right. As I was walking along with my hands in my pockets, staring at the sidewalk, half praying and half wondering what God had planned, a couple of people came to mind. One was Tom, a prominent Fort Collins businessman who is a good friend of mine, and the other was Vance, an ex-pro football player who is also a good friend of mine and Tom's.

Vance has for the last four or five years called me his spiritual big brother. We've prayed together; we've sat in church together. He's a man who was raised with a lot of abuse and has had many domestic problems in his life. We have talked often about life and love and God's will.

Vance has had unique opportunities and temptations. He hasn't always been great at handling all those situations and would be the first to tell you so. I've been privileged to be a part of his life, to help him spiritually.

So, here I was headed the long way to Linden's, looking down, thinking about my friends Tom and Vance, when I heard familiar voices. I glanced up and three feet in front of me stood the two of them, their arms around each other's shoulders, talking quietly.

I took another step and put my hands on their shoulders. They turned and, even in the street light, I could see their faces pale. "Oh, my God!" exclaimed Vance.

Tom said, "I can't believe it! Vance was just saying, 'Boy, I sure would like to see Larry tonight. I could use his help right now.'"

So I told Tom and Vance the story of turning to the right not the left. We all marveled at the timing. What was even more astounding to us was the fact that Vance had for years been telling Tom, "It's the oddest thing. Larry always shows up at just the right times in my life, those times when I most need to talk with him. It's just crazy."

I've known Tom for 10 or 12 years. He and his wife Kathleen used to take me and Tari out to dinner at the country club. He watched me go through the tragedies of paralysis and losing my family, Jack, Tari and my business. He also saw God's supernatural power sustain me through those crises.

Recently, Tom, Dary and I went to lunch. Tom told Dary, "I've known Larry for years; I've watched what's happened in his life. He's talked about how you've helped him. I want to come to your church and see what's going on over there."

Dary put his hand on Tom's shoulder. "You can come to Timberline if you want to but all I want is to play golf with you, get to know you and be your friend. If you want to come to church, fine. If you don't, we'll still be friends just the same."

Tom is not one to talk openly about spiritual things, but I know he understands what God has done and is doing in my life. And he's always been there for me as a great friend, supporter and financial advisor through the difficult times. He has respect for the ministry in which God has placed me. I see God's hand in his life.

Our friend Vance has had a lot more ups and downs than most people. Many sports heroes do have problems. It's not an excuse; it's not a cop-out. However, the fast money, the adulation and attention they get puts them in a position most people will never experience. Some handle it better than others. Vance has his troubles yet he is a wonderful person. God has his hand on Vance and will continue to work in his life. I have no doubt of that.

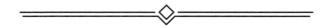

God also has his hand on Kelly (name changed), another good friend. Nikki and Kelly became friends in 1992 when they both attended CSU and danced together at the strip club in Denver.

Kelly was raised in a prominent, affluent, conservative Utah family. She didn't fall into early relationships with guys or get caught up in drugs and alcohol like a lot of people of her generation. So it was ironic she should become an exotic dancer while a college student. To this day, her folks have no idea she was once a stripper.

Some friends at CSU talked Kelly into working as a dancer. "You're away from home," they told her. "Your parents will never know. Besides, you've got the body for it and it's a quick way to pick up big bucks." She decided to give it a whirl and ended up being one of the top paid dancers at the club.

Kelly only stayed at CSU for a semester. When she got ready to leave I told her, "We'll always be in each other's lives."

She said, "Larry, I've moved around a lot and I've never kept in touch with people from my past. So I will be surprised if we do. But," she added, "I appreciate the thought and I like you a lot. Maybe we will talk again one of these days."

Instead of going home to Utah, Kelly moved to Denver and continued to dance, although she told her folks she was working at a restaurant. While in Denver she met a guy who managed one of the hottest singles bars in the area. They soon became engaged.

Kelly not only danced more and more but became part of a very fast lifestyle. The money one can make in that world is addictive, as much or more so than any drug. And Kelly was making several hundred dollars a night.

Every now and then she would call me up. I would ask, "How are you doing down there?" I was very concerned about the direction Kelly was going, further and further from her refined upbringing. Yet I knew I didn't have control over her lifestyle. I did continue to pray for her because I cared about what happened to her.

Six months after she moved to Denver, Kelly called me in the middle of the night crying. "My fiancé was killed in a motorcycle wreck last night," she sobbed. "I need to talk with you, Larry. You know how to deal with life and grief better than anyone else I know."

I realized it was a God thing I could be in Kelly's life during that difficult time. So I went to the memorial in Denver. Her parents came to town also. It was a very formal occasion and her folks were not given a clue about their daughter's occupation.

After her fiancé's death, Kelly decided to start a new life. She and a friend moved to San Diego, California. We kept in regular touch for awhile, especially by telephone. She wasn't a Christian and yet, somewhere underneath this whole thing, God was working in her life and through our friendship.

A couple of months after she moved to California, I went to visit Kelly. We had lunch, then walked on the beach and talked about what was going on with her life. She said, "I got carried away in that wild lifestyle. I was addicted to money and all that goes with it. So I've decided not to dance any more, even though I can barely make ends meet with the restaurant job I have right now."

She shrugged. "I don't know what is going to happen financially but I do know I don't want that lifestyle again." She also said she had come to realize that marrying her fast-living Denver fiancé would have been disastrous.

Kelly and I stayed in close contact for awhile. She got a job as a department manager at Nordstrom and began to look and act like the lady she was born to be. Eventually, she met a really great businessman and has a good relationship with him.

As Kelly's life stabilized, we talked less and less. But I knew we wouldn't lose touch with each other's hearts. Not long ago I prayed, "God, you know Kelly has not made a commitment to you yet. It's something I want to see happen more than anything else. Will you show me that you're still working with her and that you care about her? I know you do but will you give me a sign?"

Within a week of that prayer, Kelly called. "You know, Larry," she said, "you told me a long time ago we were always going to be in each other's lives. I guess we still are after all these years. I've been thinking about you so much the last couple of months. I want to stay in more regular contact. I want us to be a part of each other lives again. I really love you."

Kelly, who was raised Buddhist, once said to me, "Larry, I don't know anything about Christianity except things I've seen on TV and a few kooks I've met. Will you please explain it to me?" So I did.

Her response was, "That's really interesting."

I know God is still working in her heart and He's the One who prompted her to come back into my life. We have reconnected in a greater way than before because she's one of God's special projects. I'm sure of it.

I met Sandra (name changed) through mutual friends. She was from Los Angeles, in her mid-30s and Asian in appearance, with long black hair. She worked for Hewlett Packard in Fort Collins, displaying no hint of being a drug runner for gangs on the streets of LA while a young girl.

One night at dinner I shared my life story with Sandra and even felt led to tell her about my downtown ministry. She was a great listener, very interested in what I had to say. When I finished she said, "That's a touching story. I would give anything to have faith like yours and to feel the emotion you talk about. I have not been able to cry since I was a little girl."

After dinner we went dancing, then I walked her to her car which was parked in front of the salon. I got into the car to visit with her for a couple of minutes. As we were talking, she said, "That sure was a beautiful story about your life. If God would just give me some kind of sign, I would know He's real and I would become a believer, too."

Instantly, tears began to gush from her eyes. Her makeup literally slid off her face. Within moments, her blouse was soaked. I have never seen anybody cry as hard as Sandra did that night. It was like a flood and it scared her. "Maybe we should call 911!" she cried.

"You wanted a sign," I responded. "If this isn't a sign, I don't know what is."

Sandra moved out of state about a month later and I haven't had contact with her since. But I know she heard the truth of the Word that night, and I know God is active in her life.

CHAPTER 21

NEVER SAY GOODBYE

Jesus was not a religious man. In fact, He was ostracized and rejected by the religious community of His day, in part, because He hung out with sinners instead of pious people. Eventually He was rejected, persecuted and finally put to death by the religious leaders.

Why? Because He brought us unconditional love which threatened their authority and undermined their law-based belief system. There is something in our human nature that strives to put everything in a neat little box of religious rules and regulations. Those lists of dos and don'ts can cause people to become judgmental and to love conditionally, which is not love at all.

Religion leads us away from the true spirit of Jesus who was out on the streets with the sinners and the prostitutes, offering them the love they hadn't found in the "church" of their day. A good example of Jesus' unconditional love is His statement in the Bible to the woman caught in adultery. "I don't condemn you," He told her, "I give you the freedom to stop sinning."

My friend Sherri's realization that she's come to like the Jesus I've told her about is powerful because it's the way a lot of people react when they discover the real Jesus. Like the woman at the well and the woman caught in adultery, everyone is looking for love, acceptance and true friendship. Jesus' attitude toward those women, and toward us, was and is, "I don't judge you for what you've done, and I don't expect you to be perfect. Instead, I give you the freedom to quit your old ways and start new lives."

The Gospel is not about rules and regulations and church; it's about a supernatural, miraculous friendship with Jesus that doesn't require joining a church or going through religion classes. The Gospel is also about great relationships between people—supernatural, miraculous friendships.

The way to establish a relationship with Jesus is to acknowledge in your heart and mind there is a God. And to understand that God's Son, Jesus Christ, came to this earth to demonstrate His unconditional love by dying for us to pay the price for our sins.

We must tell Him, "I believe you have the power to change my life, to fill me with your supernatural love for those around me." Tell God, "Lord, I am sorry for my pride which has kept me from believing in you and accepting your love. Please forgive me and fill me with your love." He will gladly enter your life.

When you trust in God, you will receive the same love and direction my friends and I have received from God. You will be able to experience the power that has been the guiding force of my life, especially during these last few years when I have gone from the depths of tragedy to the highest heights with the incredible peace only Jesus can give.

God has been faithful in my life and in the lives of so many others. I am delighted to know I will never have to say goodbye to any of my friends who have accepted the Lord into their lives because we'll all be together in heaven throughout eternity. If you are also a believer, in the words of Jami, "I'll see you again."

Appendix A

FRIENDSHIP 101

The best term I can think of to describe the downtown outreach discussed in this book is "ministry of friendship." A ministry of friendship is showing people God's love on a daily basis. I don't always understand it nor do the people around me who have never before experienced godly love. But I am convinced that offering love and friendship has more to do with me being able to influence people for the Lord than anything else I do.

God instills love in us; we can't manufacture it. The closer we get to God through Bible reading and prayer and the more obedient we are to Him, the more He places a natural love in our heart for people around us. It seems like the more I practice showing love, the easier it is to do. And I believe what I do is possible for anyone. Every Christian should have a ministry of friendship with those God has placed in his or her life.

I am blessed to be in a visible profession where I meet hundreds of people every year. However, no matter what profession one is in, there are always people around us who are looking for God. They are looking for God in someone who will treat them better than anybody has ever treated them before. That's what Jesus did on this earth. And that's what His Spirit wants to do through our lives.

As we study God's Word and obey it, He turns us into new people old friends might not recognize. I am appalled when I compare myself now to what I used to be when I was self-serving and focused on my own agenda, using and manipulating people for my own gain. Now, when I meet people, God gives me an immediate love and concern for them.

I believe people watch other people all the time looking for everyday heroes, for people they would like to emulate, people who have peace and joy and fulfillment in their lives. Those are basic human desires. As 2 Corinthians 3:2–3 says, our Christianity is written on our hearts and people read what they see in front of them.

Jesus commanded us to live the Gospel which means "good news." How we live the Gospel determines how the people around us view Christianity. If those who know you were asked to describe you, what would they say? Would they say your life is one of good news or bad news? What would your family say? How well do you relate to your parents, your siblings, your children?

Our ability to positively affect others begins with a small but powerful word—integrity. A good definition of integrity is "what would I do if I thought nobody was looking or would ever find out?" Integrity at home, at school and on the job is crucial to friendship evangelism.

Do you constantly complain? Do you sabotage other people to get ahead? Do people like to be with you? The bottom line is this: is your school, your club, your neighborhood or your place of employment better or worse by your being there?

If we don't have a demeanor people respect, chances are they are not going to want to go to church with us either.

We need to show up on time, be dependable, set examples, not cheat the company and be peacemakers rather than gossips. In other words, we should brighten the world around us by living the Good News.

I've done a lot of training to upgrade my hair styling abilities, I go to work whether I feel like it or not, and I give my best haircut, every haircut. As a result, I have established a good reputation in Fort Collins. The more effort we put into whatever God asks us to do, the greater the results we are going to see.

It's like the guy who opened a shoe store saying, "God and I are going to be partners." But he didn't know a thing about shoes, he didn't market or advertise, and he didn't show up to work half the time. The business failed because he expected God to do everything. He didn't do his part in the partnership. So, put plenty of effort into whatever you do and God will bless that effort.

As an unmarried man, I am committed to celibacy. Not only is chastity scriptural and something I practice as an act of worship and obedience to God, I also realize people are watching me. Especially because of my social lifestyle, they want to see if I practice what I preach. But I don't push celibacy on those who don't know God and who don't make the same choices I do in life.

After checking our integrity and image, we can then look for opportunities to share Jesus with others. Before we approach unbelievers, however, we should ask ourselves, "Do I project a friendly, open attitude that makes people want to trust me as a friend?"

I believe my purpose in this world is to cause people around me to say, "I'd really like for Larry to be my friend. I know he would love me for who I am. He would be a friend to me without hidden motives."

By showing those around us we can be a true friend, we prepare their hearts for sharing the Gospel with them when the right time comes in their lives. The Bible says we are to "shine like stars." The light within us will attract others to us and to the God for whom they are unknowingly longing and searching.

If we show our friends supportive, nonjudgmental love, at some point they may ask, "How did you get that peace? What is your secret to life?" When we're asked what makes us tick, we must, and I emphasize, *slowly* check out their receptiveness to our beliefs. Oftentimes Christians pounce on unbelievers and turn them off before they have a chance to get turned on to God.

When my friends say, "You have a lot of fun, you have a lot of friends, you love to live life. What's your secret?," my response is simple. "What works for me," I tell them, "is that my views about life are based on a strong faith in God."

The phrase, "faith in God" doesn't seem to intimidate. If I say, "I believe Jesus died, was buried and three days later rose from the dead," or "I've been baptized with the Holy Spirit," or throw out some other fancy, spiritual term, they may start looking for the nearest exit.

So I say something non-threatening. And it's true—the basis for my beliefs is a strong faith in God. At that point, people often react by saying, "That's really cool," and change the subject. But, they'll file it away for future reference or, possibly, they may ask me to explain more about my faith right then.

Then I ask, "How much do you want to know? How much detail do you want me to go into?" I leave the ball in their court. I never push. I wait until their hearts, led by the Holy Spirit, are ready. I've learned to be casual in my response to questions, to be careful how I approach the subject of salvation. I try to not offend, yet let people know I'm different because of my faith.

The name of Jesus is the most powerful and controversial name in history and should be used carefully. You can talk about any religion other than Christianity and it doesn't upset non-believers. You can mention the name of any other religious leader in history without starting an argument, but the name of Jesus will make people react, either in a defensive way or in an open way.

Why is it that Jesus' name affects people so powerfully? Because, if they begin to deal with Jesus' life, including His death and resurrection, they know they'll eventually have to make a choice about how they live their lives. Down deep, people realize there are two distinct ways of living, either by basic human nature or God's way. It's either the self-absorbed, if-it-feels-good-do-it lifestyle or taking the higher path which means denying one's self and giving to others.

Although people may realize the superiority of God's plan, it scares them. They are afraid living God's way will demand discipline and commitment. Christianity may require more out of them than what they're willing to put into it.

Other terms we should use sparingly are: Christian, church, Holy Spirit, God's will, preacher, baptism, Satan, sin, religion, Scripture, tribulation, and revelation. These are just a few words that come to mind. Make a conscious effort to not use "Christianese."

I tell my friends, in the most casual way I can, that I understand many people have had a negative experience with church or with offensive, pious Christians. However, I explain, Jesus Himself was not a religious man. Unlike many tenets of today's churches, His teachings were simple and can be summed up in what He called the two greatest commandments—love the Lord your God with all your heart, soul, mind and strength; and, love your neighbor as yourself (Mark 12:30–31).

It's true. Jesus was not a religious man. He even had the nerve to suggest that loving people with the proper love is more important than religious ceremonies and traditions. The religious system that eventually put Him to death was totally against the fact that he was so down to earth, casual and laid back.

When I share this with my friends, for the first time in their lives they're not threatened by the Gospel. And they're not offended by Jesus. They think, *He sounds pretty cool, nothing like anything I've ever heard about before.* When I tell them Jesus was not religious, that's good news to them.

We should be easy-going, kind and non-threatening in our ministry of friendship. Above all, we must be led by the Lord, remaining attentive to His Spirit and to our friends' unique needs and situations. That sensitivity to God's voice comes only through daily reading and studying His Word, spending time with Him in prayer, and practicing loving the people around us every day.

God is in charge of the process, bringing our friends to a readiness to hear the Gospel and leading us to be responsive to when that moment occurs. If we're in tune with God and His leading, we'll know to go with the flow and wait for the right timing. I have learned that everybody is in a different process spiritually and on a different timetable, God's perfect timetable.

The family setting is one of the best environments in which to test our approach to love. My daughter Stephanie offers her perspective on love and friendship:

Unconditional love is something few people experience. Most have expectations put on them such as what their career should be, how much money they should make, or what kind of person they should marry. I have been very lucky in my life to have unconditional love given to me by my family. The one special person I know who will love me and listen to me no matter the issue or circumstance is my dad, Larry Baker.

I have been able to view my father from many different angles. I have seen him make major changes in his life and get to the point where what made him happy was filling a void in other peoples' lives and loving them in a way no one else had. God has given him a special love for others. It is not always easy to love your own children unconditionally and, in fact, some people don't; but to love a total stranger unconditionally is definitely extraordinary.

During a confused time in my life, I turned to my dad. He opened up all he had to me and took me in. I know what he did for me is something he would do for anyone else with the same need. I was able to live with him and see him in a light I had never seen before. At first I didn't understand what was happening in his life, but I got to meet many of the people in this book and witness their life changes.

I know God has given Dad a special mission which serves many purposes. The gift he has is not only a blessing to the people it affects directly, but people he comes into contact with day by day sense there is something unique about him. People who just see him downtown doing his daily rounds are touched by the fact he always has a smile and he's always there.

It has not always been easy for my father, and it has not always been easy for me to see the things life has thrown at him, but I know the love God gives him for people around him is what keeps him going. I am blessed to have his unconditional love in my life and I am proud to say many other people are too.

I have struggled with religion all of my life. The most comforting thing to me is knowing God's love is unconditional love. If everyone loved without judgment the way my dad does through God, many lives would be changed.

Isn't it true our whole lives are a search for love? All we have to do to show people God has all the love they will ever need is to love them unconditionally with His love. It's so simple.

Stephanie Baker Perry

Appendix B

PERSONAL NOTES

On tragedy

I don't believe everyone has to go through the pain I experienced to be used of God. Through tragedy, I learned to appreciate things I had taken for granted for years and to recognize God is always faithful. I learned to depend on Him instead of my own abilities to work out everything for myself. The traumatic episodes of my life taught me to trust Him for the next steps in my life, so I would cut down the odds of making future mistakes.

About beautiful people

For whatever reason, God has brought lots of attractive people into my life. Actually, they're a spiritually neglected group because others assume they have everything. I happen to work in a glamour business in a fast-paced, exciting, college town where there are lots of young, good-looking people, especially in the downtown area. God has given me favor with those folks. I don't question it; that's just the way it is. We should all bloom where we're planted.

Regarding romantic relationships

Even though I was tempted to get into another relationship after Tari left, and although I wanted to have someone special like her as a companion, what God was doing in my life and the peace I had in my heart was more valuable to me than relief from loneliness. I knew such an alliance could cause more pain and take me several steps backwards from who He wanted me to be.

When I realized peace was more important than a temporary escape and that I didn't need unnecessary pain in my life, that was a turning point for me. I tell other singles, "When the peace is more important than the pain, then you will have turned a corner in your walk with God and your contentment in life."

On friendship

I'm not out in Old Town, my pockets stuffed with Gospel tracts, trying to put notches on my Bible. That's not what I do. What I do is try to make as many friends as I can and be a friend people can count on.

When I meet someone new and they want to go to a movie or go shoot pool, I'm not chomping at the bit thinking, *When can I talk to them about the Lord?* Instead, I work on establishing a friendship with them. That's my goal for everyone I meet. I want to become a good friend to them.

Today's church often approaches the question, "How do we win the world?" similar to the question, "How do we sell vacuum cleaners?" To me, it's not like that at all.

Sharing Jesus by loving people and making new friends doesn't require sales techniques. It should be as natural as breathing. And it makes me so happy when people say, "You're the best friend I've ever had" or, "You've helped me to know the Lord better than I ever did before."

About encouragement

Every Christian should have the gift of encouragement. If it's not a well-developed gift, we should work on developing it. Fortunately for me, my dad, who was a popular barber and a role model, was friendly and encouraging. People used to say he could move his barbershop to a phone booth and everyone would still go to him for haircuts.

I once asked my dad the secret of his successful businesses. In his simple, straightforward manner, Dad responded, "I treat the customer in my chair better than he's been treated in any other barber's chair." He also said, "Don't just take flowers to a person's funeral. Give them flowers while they're alive."

If you look, you can find characteristics you like about people and tell them so. Cheap flattery doesn't work; it's an insult. The more I've developed spiritually, the more I look at people the way I looked at Nikki the first night we went out. I saw beyond the stripper with the tough exterior to a wonderful woman with a big heart. I saw a lovable, dynamic person who had hidden those great traits behind the walls she'd built. As we progressed in our friendship, at appropriate times, I could point out things I liked about her.

Sherri is a good example of the power of encouragement. She has a great smile and every time we got together, I would say, "With that smile, you can get anything you want!" The more I told her that, the more she wanted to smile.

She's one of the best waitresses in town, if not the best. No matter what kind of a day she's having, she can wait on eight tables at a time and keep that smile on her face. She makes everybody feel special and, as a result, makes good tips. I've told her, "If you carry that attitude into every area of your life, not just turn it on for the tips at the restaurant, you'll have a happy and successful life."

I try to say encouraging things to people like, "You know, you're really good at that," "I really appreciate this about you," or, "You make me feel really good about this." And, "I like you." When I was in elementary school, if we wanted to make a friend at school, we either wrote a little note or we said, "I like you. Will you play with me?"

Thank goodness I've been able to knock down the walls of adulthood and go back to the childlike behavior of being able to walk up to someone, look in their face and say, "I like you. I want to be around you. Would you like to spend time with me?"

Encouragement is something all Christians should practice. If we search for things we love about our friends and tell them we like those traits, they'll feel good about themselves. Because we live in a society that from birth dampens self-esteem, it's a breath of fresh air when people say things such as, "I like this about you," or "You should do more of that because you're good at it." Being an encourager is an important facet of developing long-term, loving relationships.

Regarding obedience

This book is a product of obedience. During the years God was guiding me from tragedy to triumph, I had no idea I would someday be sharing those experiences in written form. But, one day as I was cutting Becky Lyles' hair and telling her about my latest downtown adventure, she said, "Sounds like you should write a book, Larry."

I laughed and replied, "Well, maybe when I'm sitting in my rocker on the front porch with nothin' else to do."

I didn't think anything more about the conversation until several weeks later when Becky and her husband Steve suggested we write the book together. I thanked them for their obedience to the prompting of the Holy Spirit and we took off on the exciting endeavor of co-authoring this manuscript.

Another exciting result of obedience is the recent formation of a GenX church in Old Town. The parent church, Timberline, saw the need for a church in Fort Collins specifically geared to those in the young adult age range. As a result, Joshua's Crossing was birthed in 1999 and has been well received in Old Town. I'm pleased to now have two contemporary church settings where I can take my downtown friends and where they can find acceptance, love and an upbeat style of music and preaching.

Obedience comes in different forms because each person is a unique individual with a distinct personality and influence on those around him or her. However, the one thing we all have in common is that we're each supposed to make a difference in our world.

My prayer is that you will be all God wants you to be and find the joy of being a special friend to many people. Remember, obedience brings blessing, passion for living, friendship and unprecedented adventure.

Whoops, my pager just went off again. I'm outa here!

—Lar

APPENDIX C

SUGGESTED READING

Books for Those Who Are Not Yet Believers

Case for Christ, Lee Strobel
Zondervan Publishing House

More Than a Carpenter, Josh McDowell
Tyndale House Publishers

The Journey: A Bible for Seeking God & Understanding Life
New International Version
Zondervan Publishing House

The Jesus I Never Knew, Philip Yancey
Zondervan Publishing House

The Unknown God, Alister McGrath
Wm. B. Eerdmans Publishing

God's Story, Anne Graham Lotz
Word Publishing

Books for New Believers

Following Jesus, Douglas Shaw w/Bayard Taylor
Gospel Light Publications

Walk This Way, Tim Woodroof
NavPress

New Christian's Handbook, Max Anders
Thomas Nelson Publishers

Life Essentials: A Guide for Spiritual Growth
Moody Press

Fresh Faith, Jim Cymbala w/Dean Merrill
Zondervan Publishing House

Experiencing God, Henry Blackaby & Claude King
Broadman & Holman Publishers

Books for Those Who Want to Help Others Become Believers

How to Give Away Your Faith, Paul Little
InterVarsity Press

Conspiracy of Kindness, Steve Sjogren
Vine Books

Friendship Evangelism by the Book, Tom Stebbins
Christian Publications

Life-Style Evangelism, Joe Aldrich
Multnomah Books

Out of the Salt Shaker, Rebecca M. Pippert
InterVarsity Press

Gentle Persuasion, Joe Aldrich
Multnomah Press

Lifestyle Discipleship, Jim Petersen
NavPress

Inside the Mind of Unchurched Harry & Mary
Lee Strobel & Bill Hybels
Zondervan Publishing House

Sharing Jesus, Douglas Shaw
Gospel Light Publications

Becoming a Contagious Christian, Bill Hybels et al
Zondervan Publishing House

Fresh Wind, Fresh Fire, Jim Cymbala & Dean Merrill
Zondervan Publishing House

Living Proof: Sharing Jesus Naturally, Jim Petersen
NavPress

To order additional copies of

It's a God Thing!

Please send $11.95* plus $2.95 shipping and handling to:

(Wyoming residents: Please add 5.0% Sales Tax)

LBL Productions
PO Box 314
Cheyenne, WY 82003

*Quantity discounts are available.

Call: 970-221-4983